# The Seven Wonders of the Inland Waterways

John Suggitt

CANALBOOKSHOP

# The Seven Wonders of the
# Inland Waterways

## John Suggitt

Published 2019
Canal Book Shop
Audlem Mill  The Wharf  Audlem  Cheshire  CW3 0DX

ISBN 978-1-9160125-1-6

# Contents

The author wishes to thank Dr. Andrew J. Suggitt
for his inspiration during the writing of this book.

# Introduction

For those unfamiliar with the inland waterways network serving England and Wales, there follows a brief history of its construction, growth, decline, and restoration. This is to help the reader gain an appreciation of how the Seven Wonders provided a vital means of raising the profile of the canal network during a critical stage in its history.

Prior to industrialisation, the majority of Britain's heavier goods had been transported by river for centuries, primarily because this load is borne by the water rather than a truck or carriage, saving a huge amount of effort (Figure 1).

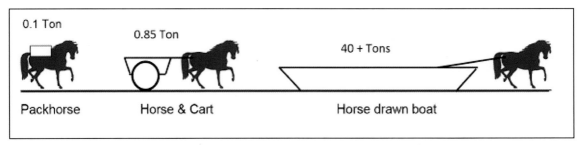

**Figure 1**   Different ways of transporting goods in the 18th century

The development of our canals to improve and connect these rivers gained momentum in the 18th century, with our civil engineers taking their lead from the French, who already had successful canals in operation. Within England and Wales, the majority of canal construction occurred between 1766 and 1835, peaking around 1792. A notable exception to this is the Manchester Ship Canal, a large-scale undertaking that occurred during the late nineteenth century. The early canals offered major benefits, most notably a substantial reduction in transport costs. For example, before the canals, the excessive costs associated with the transportation of coal meant a fourfold difference in the unit cost of this commodity between the pitheads in Leicestershire and the ever expanding market in London (Figure 2 overleaf).

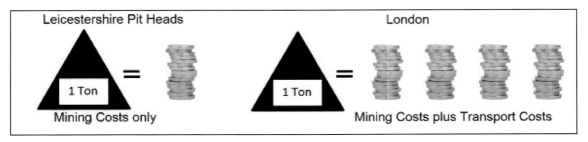

**Figure 2** The effect of transport costs on the price of coal prior to the arrival of the canals

The advantages of canals were especially pronounced in industrial areas lacking efficient transport links, such as the West Midlands, where the manufacture of iron was undertaken, and north west England, a centre of textile manufacture. Canals acted as an effective means of transporting raw materials to or within these regions, as a consistent source of water for manufacturing processes, and as a means of transporting the finished goods from the manufacturing sites. In short, they were both a driver and a beneficiary of large scale industrial growth, and as such their history is entwined. England's canals were developed around a central feature called 'The Cross', which consisted of canals linking four major rivers: the Thames, the Severn, the Mersey and the Trent. To this day, 'The Cross' (Figure 3) serves as the backbone of the canal network, connecting England's industrial cities. Subsequent canals were built around this backbone to create the more extensive inland waterway network we have today.

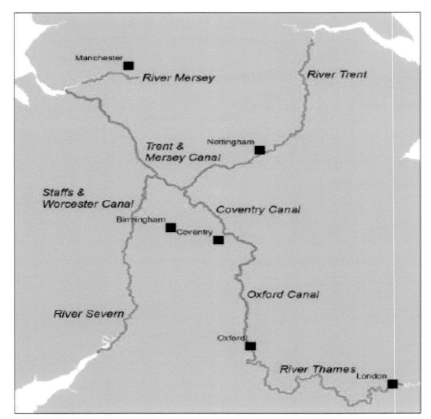

**Figure 3**

The canals of 'The Cross'

N.B. The Bridgewater Canal provides a five mile link between Preston Brook where the Trent & Mersey Canal terminates, and the Mersey Estuary (the remainder of this waterway is omitted for clarity).

# Introduction

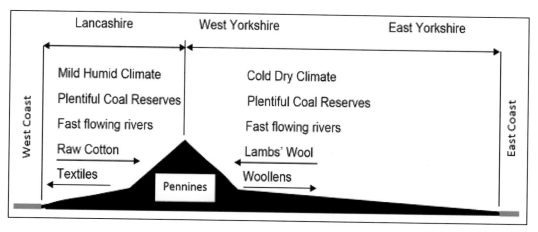

**Figure 4**  The factors which accelerated canal construction within northern England

Figure 4 indicates the reasons for canal construction on both sides of the Pennines. The high humidity on the Lancashire side offered ideal conditions for cotton spinning, whilst the plentiful supply of wool on the Yorkshire side had led to the manufacture of woollen cloth. Developments in manufacturing techniques meant that by the late 18th century, production on both sides of the Pennines was expanding rapidly: the demand for workers in woollen manufacture resulted in a doubling of the population of Leeds between 1770 and 1800, also the number of cotton mills in Manchester grew from two in 1790 to sixty six in 1821. This rapid expansion presented new challenges for the industry located in northern England. Raw cotton was imported into Lancashire from America, but landward transportation proved difficult as the mills were sited on rivers which were only partially navigable. Initially, the wool merchants in west Yorkshire sourced their wool from local shepherds, despite Pennine sheep yielding only coarse wool. They were shrewd enough to realise that finer wool was available from milder climes located within areas further afield, and later arranged for supplies from areas such as Lincolnshire and Norfolk. Thus, the transportation of raw materials made up a rising proportion of input costs as these industries developed, together with an increased need for reliable and abundant supplies of water. Canals answered many of these problems, resulting in their construction extending from 'The Cross' throughout the midlands and into the Pennine region.

The huge cost savings to be made by 'canalisation' ensured that this expansion was rapid, though like any well-used transport network, congestion soon became a problem. Lock flights, where boats have to pause whilst locks empty or fill with water to the required level, became particularly notorious bottlenecks. Within rural Cheshire, lock flights along a section of the Trent and Mersey Canal linking the Potteries with the Mersey estuary were duplicated in an attempt to avoid delays. In areas of Birmingham, this approach was not possible due to the close proximity of factories and other infrastructure, leading to gas lighting being employed, thereby permitting 24 hour operation. Ultimately even this was not enough to reduce congestion, and an alternative route was constructed to bypass these busy lengths of canal, a solution geographically similar to the modern day M6 Toll motorway.

During their heyday, the canals were constructed, owned and operated by a proliferation of private companies, almost all of which were highly profitable. The tolls extracted for passage were large, and none more so than the Loughborough Navigation Company, which linked London and much of the east Midlands with the River Trent. In 1833, the company paid an annual dividend of some 108%, and the market value of a £142 share was a princely £1,240! Ultimately the rich cash reserves of this company drove the development of the Midland Railway, which replaced the canal as the primary means of transportation - a trend repeated more broadly. Thus many of the companies which built and operated the canals ultimately brought about their demise; see also Footnote. The development of the quicker and more efficient railways began a gradual reduction in canal traffic and much of the waterway network spiralled into decline. The rapid expansion of the railways in the late nineteenth and early twentieth century accelerated this trend. By the end of the Second World War, little remained of what was once a thriving network, some canals having been closed to traffic entirely. Thankfully the

decline of the canals was not terminal, and as the post-WW2 economic boom took hold, opportunities for leisure time increased, enabling waterways enthusiasts to notice the sorry state of the canals and the fate of the people who worked on them. Tom Rolt (Figure 5), an accomplished mechanical engineer originally from Chester, was so enthusiastic about the surviving canals that he fitted out a narrow boat in order that he and his wife could undertake a pre-WW2 cruise around the waterways of the midlands and North Wales, where he was so moved by the manner in which the longstanding culture of the canal folk was being cast aside, that

**Figure 5**

Tom Rolt, engineer, author, canal and steam railway enthusiast, co-founder of the Inland Waterways Association
*Angela Rolt, courtesy of Rolt Collection*

he recorded his findings in a book entitled *Narrow Boat*. This work, together with his later book *Green & Silver* describing a voyage on board a hire cruiser along many of the Irish rivers and canals, offered an authentic insight into the state of these inland waterways at that time, thereby making more people aware of their plight.

Robert Aickman, a London publicist who was not blessed with Rolt's practical skills, was equally committed to the waterways. Realising that if the canal system was to be saved, he decided to promote the benefits of maintaining the network to all who would listen. His book *The Story of Our Inland Waterways* (1955) was an attempt to acquaint people with precisely what our canals had to offer, and why we should strive to preserve them. Other than their passion for our canals, Aickman and Rolt had little else in common, but their shared interest was strong enough for them to found the Inland Waterways Association (IWA) in 1946: a body dedicated to the preservation of the canal network which to this day remains active (currently the membership stands at around 14,000). In order to raise the profile of the canals, Robert Aickman identified the '**Seven Wonders of the Waterways**' (Figures 6 & 7): a series of remarkable engineering features that provided novel solutions to some of the major difficulties encountered by our engineers during the design, building and operation of our canals. Five of the Seven Wonders are located in northern England; here, the difficult terrain

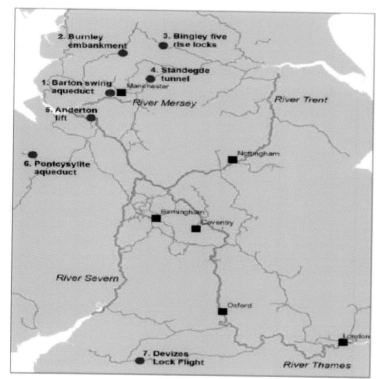

**Figure 6**

The location of the Seven Wonders of the British canal network

(N.B. this numbering is entirely random and does not imply an order of magnitude or importance.)

required unique and often spectacular engineering solutions. The Seven Wonders offer examples of the finest civil engineering practices of the day, with five being built during the peak of canal construction in the late 18th and early to mid-19th centuries.

A further two Wonders arrived a few decades later - the Anderton Boat Lift (1875) and the Barton Swing Aqueduct (1893) - each of which embodied mechanical engineering principles in their design, requiring hydraulics in order to function. Both of these structures have been updated during their working lives, reflecting later developments in the fields of both mechanical and electrical engineering (see Chapters 1 and 5). The approach to 'market' the canals as a leisure activity worked, and throughout the 1950s and 1960s, canals began to capture people's imaginations around the country. A culture of canal 'cruising' grew up, where enthusiasts would buy and renovate old narrow boats (or lighter, easier to handle 'cruisers') and sail them at the weekend. Also, the hiring of canal boats for one or two weeks' duration became popular during the summer months. In order to further their objectives, the IWA decided to hold their first Boat Rally at Market Harborough in Leicestershire in 1950; see Figure 8. The aim was to 'showcase' the inland waterways, thereby introducing a plan for both their restoration and upkeep. Though the success of this event exceeded all expectations, attracting 120 boats and 50,000 visitors, it created an irreparable rift between Rolt and Aickman. Whilst the Boat Rally was Rolt's

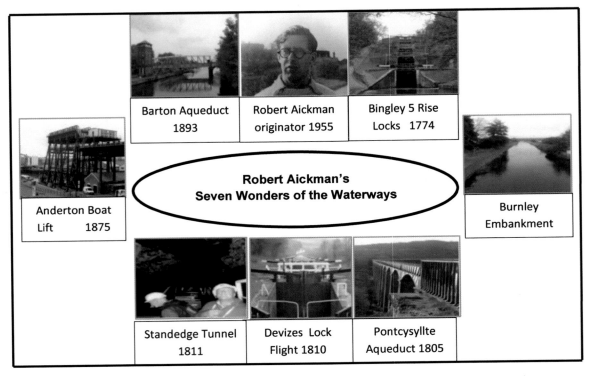

**Figure 7** Robert Aickman's 'Seven Wonders of the Waterways'

idea, Aickman had taken it upon himself to promote it in a manner which would appeal to a far wider audience, apparently without Rolt's knowledge. Perhaps at this juncture, Rolt decided that his efforts might be better appreciated elsewhere. Shortly afterwards, he sold his narrow boat and parted company with the IWA, whereupon he became the driving force in the preservation and restoration of the narrow gauge Talyllyn steam railway located in Mid Wales, an undertaking which has proven to be very successful to the present day. Nevertheless, the increasing popularity of boating meant that the hobby caught on, and boat rallies have been a fixture of the boating calendar ever since. Numerous important rallies were held throughout the 1950s and 60s, notably at Stratford upon Avon in 1964 where the Queen Mother was in attendance to witness the successful restoration of the Southern Stratford Canal, and subsequently at Blackburn in 1965, where the guests included the local MP Barbara Castle. Later in that year a Government reshuffle saw Mrs Castle (who some years later became Baroness Castle of Blackburn) assume the role of Transport Minister. Thus, the waterways gained a very useful ally, whose mind-set was no doubt influenced by her positive experience of a thriving waterway a few months earlier! The 1966 National Rally held at Marple, see Figure 8, highlighted the poor condition of both the Lower Peak Forest and Ashton Canals, each of which was unnavigable at the time. One of the campaigners of the day coined the phrase 'The Cheshire Ring': a circular route around the county within which these waterways were

**Figure 8**   Plaques from the IWA National Boat Rallies held at Market Harborough, Leicestershire, in 1950 and Marple, Greater Manchester, in 1966

mostly located. This captured the imagination of many sympathisers, resulting in major restoration initiatives such as 'Operation Ashton' in 1968 and 'Ashtac' in 1972 employing some of the largest mobilisations of volunteers in British peacetime, where thousands of enthusiasts worked together.

As restoration gained in popularity, it became increasingly organised; so-called mobile restoration volunteer groups were deployed resulting in the founding of the Waterways Recovery Group which was spearheaded by the avid waterways enthusiast Graham

Palmer, who in an attempt to coordinate canal restoration nationwide, edited a broadsheet publication called *Navvies Notebook*. The Waterways Recovery Group, which emerged as a sister group to the IWA, remains to this day at the forefront of canal restoration nationwide. Though initially British Waterways, who at the time controlled most canals, displayed hostility to this pragmatic 'hands-on' organisation, attitudes softened throughout the 1960s and eventually volunteers began to be welcomed rather than shunned. Thankfully, the Canal & River Trust, the organisation which has now succeeded British Waterways, enjoys a cordial relationship with WRG, recognising their professionalism and competence, on some occasions working hand in glove on restoration projects to their mutual benefit.

The popularity of boat rallies and canal restoration held up through the 1970s, 80s, 90s and 2000s, suggesting that boating for leisure has never been more popular. The present day total length of navigable waterways - approximately 3500km (2200 miles) - is certainly the largest since the early 19th century heyday of canals. However, today's canal network faces a number of challenges, including a loss of Central Government funding, an ageing volunteer workforce and a rise in the availability of alternative leisure activities amongst younger adults. If the waterway network is to survive and prosper, it needs to be promoted to new and perhaps younger audiences, which is what this book attempts to do.

# Chapter 1

# Barton Swing Aqueduct
## (Bridgewater Canal - Manchester Ship Canal)

During 1761, the pioneer British canal engineer James Brindley completed the initial section of the Bridgewater Canal in order to transport coal from the mines at Worsley to Stretford some five miles away, where it was offloaded for transfer by road to nearby Manchester; see Figure 9. The centrepiece of this first section of canal was a fixed three arch masonry aqueduct over the Mersey and Irwell Navigation at Barton, to the west of Manchester, this structure being unprecedented within Britain at that instant in time, see Figure 10. The novelty of seeing loaded boats passing over the aqueduct, as well as beneath it, attracted sightseers in large numbers.

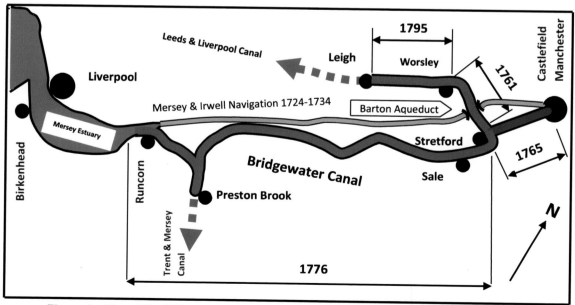

**Figure 9**  Plan of the Bridgewater Canal, indicating the stages in which it was constructed

**Figure 10**

James Brindley's fixed aqueduct at Barton, the left hand arch used for navigation

Brindley's fixed aqueduct enabled the Bridgewater Canal both to develop as a separate entity to the Mersey and Irwell Navigation (flowing beneath it), and eventually when the Canal was extended westward to Runcorn, to compete with it. The fixed aqueduct remained in use until 1892, and may well have stood until this day had it not been necessary to demolish it, on the grounds that it offered insufficient clearance beneath to enable much larger sea going vessels to navigate the Manchester Ship Canal, which later employed much of the route of the Mersey and Irwell Navigation. Subsequently in 1887, the Ship Canal Company bought out the Bridgewater Canal at a cost of £1,710,000. The value of the cheque made out to complete this purchase broke all previous records.

The principal engineer for the Ship Canal was Edward Leader Williams, a former employee of the Weaver Navigation and later the Bridgewater Canal, who, no doubt mindful of its obligations, designed a swing aqueduct at Barton consisting of a steel frame which houses a cast iron trough some 72 metres (235 feet) long by 5 metres (16 feet) wide, the moving structure weighing 1472 tonnes (1450 tons), plus an additional 812 tonnes (800 tons) when in water. This movable aqueduct has proven to be a very effective replacement for Brindley's original fixed structure. The contractor engaged in the construction of the swing aqueduct was Andrew Handyside and Company of Derby, whose attributes proved to be ideally suited to this daunting task. Interestingly the company was managed by Scotsman Andrew Handyside, a close relative of the Baird family who collectively were responsible for the construction of the principal canals within lowland Scotland. Early in his career, Andrew had worked for his uncle Charles Baird who managed the Baird Company based in St Petersburg, which undertook iron founding, bridge building and steamship manufacture.

Figure 11 shows the Swing Aqueduct nearing completion, with Brindley's fixed aqueduct in front of it being dismantled. The two structures had co-existed in order to minimise the disruption to the heavy traffic then using the Bridgewater Canal.

**Figure 11**   Barton Swing Aqueduct viewed from the west whilst under construction

Not only was the Handyside Company a prolific bridge builder, having erected 400 bridges for the London, Brighton and South Coast Railway between 1840 and 1846, it also had a reputation for undertaking work in constrained areas, whilst satisfying demanding customer deadlines, which it achieved by pre-assembling and testing the completed structures within its yard sited on the banks of the River Derwent. This mode of operation was absolutely crucial when one considers that it was not possible to operate the swing aqueduct until Brindley's fixed structure had been demolished. Eventually the first barge navigated the swing aqueduct in 1893 prior to its formal opening in 1894.

The Handyside Company was responsible for many of the other structures along the Ship Canal including Barton Road swing bridge, this also being a replacement of a fixed structure. Both moving structures here are supported from a common purpose built central island, each swinging structure resting on a thrust bearing (Figure 12, overleaf) employing sixty four cast iron taper rollers with a nominal diameter of 356 millimetres (14 inches) housed within an 8.23 metres (27 feet) diameter race. This arrangement offers the highest possible load carrying capacity within the area available.

During assembly, the taper roller thrust bearing would require the use of the jib cranes shown in Figure 12 in order to handle the heavier components, many of which were riveted together on site.

Though at the time, steel was emerging as a useful engineering material, the Handyside Company concentrated on improving the strength of cast iron. For example, it is claimed that these improvements gave an increase of between 17% and 35% in its tensile strength. This

**Figure 12** The taper roller thrust bearing during assembly

development work was highly significant in the case of these moving structures, where some of the cast iron components employed were being loaded very close to their absolute limits. These major Ship Canal structures are inspected regularly by a team of resident engineers, who in 1928 identified pronounced distortion of the cast iron taper rollers within the thrust bearing serving the aqueduct. At this time these rollers were replaced by a set manufactured in steel.

The steel taper rollers now in use are visible behind the safety rails between the fixed masonry support plinth and the movable circular base, whose curved rack (see Figure

13) is obscured by its guard which protrudes to the left, just below the tree branches. The widespread use of riveted joints employed throughout the construction is evident both here and in the later Figures 16 and 17. Bearing in mind the size of the structure, this technique would have permitted assembly to be undertaken both 'off site' and 'on site' as required by the Handyside Company.

**Figure 13** The present day steel support rollers serving the aqueduct's thrust bearing

The hydraulic systems employed in the operation of both the swing aqueduct and the road swing bridge (see Figure 14) were designed and installed by the Armstrong Mitchell Company of Newcastle, which had extensive experience in the design and construction of maritime and dock facilities; consequently in 1889 it had provided the hydraulics for Tower Bridge, London. The company head, Sir William George Armstrong, who himself was very experienced in the design and applications of this type of machinery, had earlier patented the hydraulic accumulator to accommodate widely fluctuating system loads, whilst constructing a hydraulic crane on the side of the Humber.

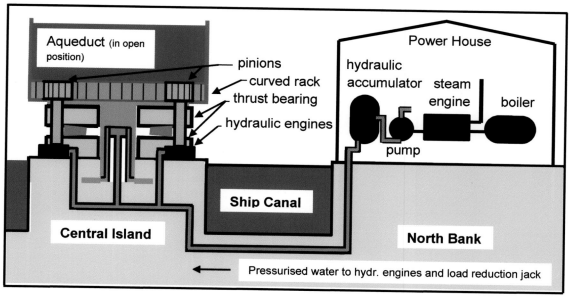

**Figure 14**  Schematic drawing of hydraulic circuit serving Barton Swing Aqueduct as built

The swing aqueduct and the road swing bridges are operated by hydraulic engines (see Figure 15) located on the central island, relying originally upon a power house sited on the north bank. The pumps were driven by steam engines, which in turn employed two Lancashire boilers to raise the quantity of steam required. A novel means of reducing the pressure on the thrust bearing was employed in the form of hydraulic jacking, which was designed to halve the downward load when the structures were swung (see Figure 14). This idea proved to be so successful that it was employed on some of the swing bridges serving road crossings elsewhere on the Ship Canal.

In 1939, the Armstrong Mitchell hydraulic engines were replaced with a pair of three cylinder radial engines supplied by the Hydraulic Engineering Company of Chester.

During 1940, a new power house was erected on the central island incorporating electrically powered hydraulic pumps, see Figures 16, 17 and 18, the new arrangement offering a far more efficient use of both space and energy. The original north bank power house complex now redundant, was later demolished during the 1940s.

**Figure 15**  The Armstrong Mitchell Hydraulic Engines serving Barton Road Swing Bridge

A surviving part of the north abutment of Brindley's fixed aqueduct is visible to the left of Figure 17, and again in Figure 18 amidst the trees immediately to the left of the swing aqueduct, thus bearing testimony to the longevity of Brindley's workmanship.

**Figure 16**  Barton Swing Aqueduct viewed looking east from Barton Road Swing Bridge

**Figure 17**  Barton Swing Aqueduct seen from the north bank of the Manchester Ship Canal

**Figure 18**  Barton Road Swing Bridge and Swing Aqueduct seen from the south bank of the Manchester Ship Canal. The power house is positioned between the two bridges it serves

**Figure 19** The Bridgewater Canal looking south towards Trafford Park and Stretford from a point close to the commencement of the Barton Swing Aqueduct

The line of the canal employed when exiting James Brindley's original fixed aqueduct, in the direction of Trafford Park (see Figure 19), would have run from a point near to this end of the railing to the immediate left of the bush in the foreground. A diversion was necessary here, which would have been introduced shortly before the swing aqueduct was opened. The towpath reverted to the present layout when Brindley's fixed structure was demolished. The craft approaching in the distance is a trip boat, possibly headed for Worsley. To the right of this vessel the bridge enables the towpath to pass over the entrance to one of the many arms serving the numerous factories located in Trafford Park, which was formerly one of the world's largest industrial estates.

Surprisingly, on Sundays this neighbourhood often has a somewhat 'rural' feel to it despite the heavily urbanised surroundings. Towards the end of 2015 when this photograph was taken, affordable housing was under construction in this vicinity, which lies very close to the giant Trafford Centre shopping complex.

In addition to the three arches employed in Brindley's original masonry aqueduct shown in Figure 10, a fourth arch had been built immediately to the north in order to cross Barton

Lane which ran parallel with what was then Mersey and Irwell Navigation. Around 1893, during the construction of the swing aqueduct, the line of the Bridgewater Canal was duplicated slightly further east. At this time, the Barton Lane underpass was widened requiring a new but somewhat utilitarian steel aqueduct to be employed, and subsequently the original masonry aqueduct was dismantled. Thankfully the local authority, Eccles Corporation, which was involved with this work had the foresight to arrange for one of the portals of the original masonry aqueduct to be rebuilt nearby on the end of the now truncated section of canal; see Figure 20. This early attempt at conservation offers an everlasting impression of how Brindley's original three arch masonry aqueduct would have looked, and late in 2015 this initiative won a long overdue Heritage Transport Award.

On 21 May 1894, shortly after the Barton Swing Aqueduct was introduced (thereby permitting the Manchester Ship Canal to be opened), Edward Leader Williams, who had now become its Chief Engineer, was knighted.

**Figure 20** The present day steel aqueduct used by the Bridgewater Canal to cross Barton Lane was built to the east of the original crossing. After dismantling, one of the portals of the original masonry aqueduct was rebuilt on the end of the original canal line, thus offering a commendable approach to heritage well ahead of its time.

Thanks to the sequence of events that unfolded here from the late eighteenth until the end of the nineteenth centuries, which in themselves span the vast majority of the canal building era in England and Wales, the Barton Swing Aqueduct offers a fitting introduction to the Seven Wonders of the inland waterways. Undoubtedly, in its heyday, the original James Brindley fixed masonry aqueduct would have been a 'Canal Wonder' in its own right.

# Chapter 2

# Burnley Embankment
## (Leeds and Liverpool Canal)

This embankment is a dead straight length of canal extending for almost a mile, passing close to the town centre of Burnley, Lancashire above the roof tops of many of the houses. To fully appreciate the reasons for its existence, one has to delve into the history of the Leeds and Liverpool Canal, one of the longest and arguably, in terms of revenue, one of the most successful of the English canals.

Following much debate over its route, construction began simultaneously at both ends during late 1770, in order to achieve its two main objectives which were to transport coal westward to Liverpool, and limestone eastward to Bradford and Leeds. The original route for the canal, agreed in 1770, passed through Whalley in Lancashire, with branches serving the towns of Blackburn and Burnley; see Figure 21. This route was perceived to be the most direct line from Yorkshire to Liverpool, hence strongly favoured by those proprietors based on the east side of the Pennines. By 1777, Liverpool was linked to the coalfields in the Wigan area, whilst Leeds and Bradford were linked to the limestone quarries in the Craven district located to the east of the Pennine summit. Thus, despite the through route remaining unfinished, the canal promoters had already realised their initial objectives. At this time, the nation's economy was adversely affected by the American War of Independence; consequently the funding ran out and construction was paused for thirteen years.

As a direct consequence, the towns in north west England engaged in textile manufacture were starved of raw materials, thus they were greatly affected by what came to be known as the 'cotton famine' resulting in much hardship among the working people throughout the region. Though funds were unavailable and many of the local industries were unable to function, this interruption proved to be of great benefit to the canal company, and

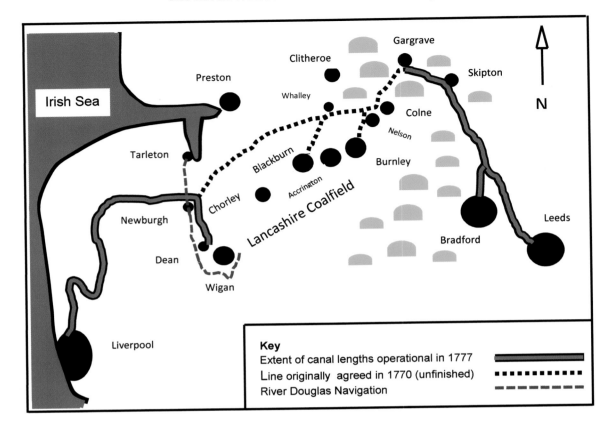

**Figure 21**   The extent of the Leeds Liverpool Canal in 1777 when construction
ceased for a period of thirteen years due to lack of funding

subsequently the local population, in that it offered the proprietors the opportunity to 'take stock' and contemplate as to how they may best complete their venture.

Upon resumption of construction, with a far harsher financial climate in place, and following much shareholder discussion, the more southerly route proposed by the Liverpool based surveyor Peter Perez Burdett was adopted (see Figure 22), directly linking the east Lancashire towns of Wigan, Chorley, Blackburn, Accrington, Burnley and Nelson, and virtually remaining within the confines of the Lancashire coalfield, thereby offering the scope for much 'short haul' trade which proved to be lucrative, hence was to continue to well into the twentieth century. Had the canal been constructed to the line originally agreed, passing through Whalley (see Figure 21), the towns of Burnley and Nelson (formerly known as Marsden) would have been served by an arm terminating on the north side of the Calder Valley. Thus it would not have been necessary to construct the Burnley Embankment, thereby denying us this truly outstanding example of eighteenth century civil engineering.

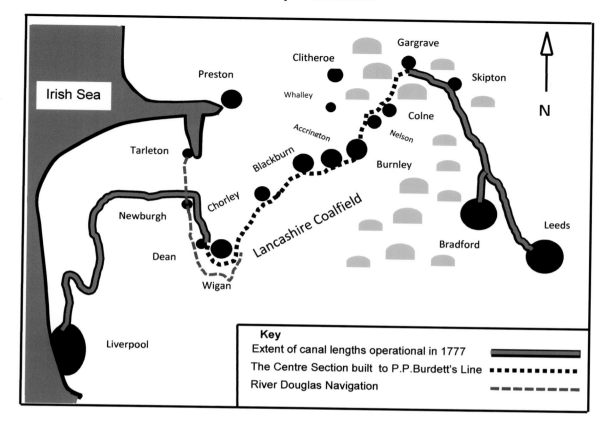

**Figure 22** The revised route of the centre section of the Canal adopted when construction recommenced around 1790

As a result of the revised route, the Lancashire end of the canal is a series of lengthy pounds interrupted by lock flights (Figure 23), presenting the canal engineers with some very difficult challenges. The 37km (23 mile) length of canal extending through undulating terrain from Blackburn to Nelson, known locally as the 'Burnley Pool', was required at one stage to cross the valley of the (Lancashire) River Calder which was without doubt the most difficult obstacle to overcome during this phase of construction. It was not until 1795 that Robert Whitworth, the accomplished canal engineer and one time assistant to James Brindley, produced the specifications for this work, which entailed the creation of the Burnley Embankment spanning a distance of around 1.6km (1 mile) with a maximum height of 12.2 metres (40 feet). Robert Whitworth had been encouraged by his colleague and fellow Brindley confidant John Longbotham to construct the Leeds and Liverpool as a broad canal, this decision having huge significance in the design, cost and building of the embankment. Apart from its physical size, construction difficulties were further hampered by the close proximity to working coal mines which resulted in settlement after its completion. This factor, together with the enormity of the structure, resulted in a Terminus Warehouse (Figure 24) being erected close to the south end of the

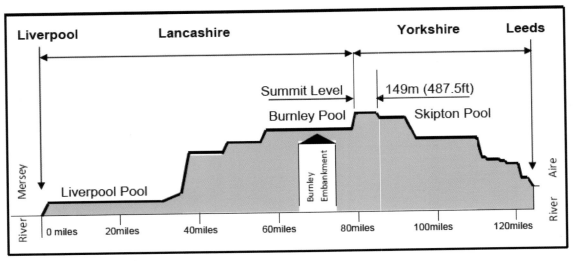

**Figure 23** A sectional view of the Leeds and Liverpool Canal indicating the 'Burnley Pool'

embankment in order to accommodate the transfer of goods between the nascent waterway and the nearby road until the canal was fully opened as a through route on Saturday 18 October 1816.

During 2016, as part of the Leeds and Liverpool canal bi-centenary celebrations, the original maiden voyage along its full length was replicated employing the traditional short boat *Kennet* (see Footnote, also Figures 101 & 102) with her crew resplendent in period attire. Many canal side locations used this opportunity to showcase their heritage, including an area of Burnley between the canal embankment and the area around

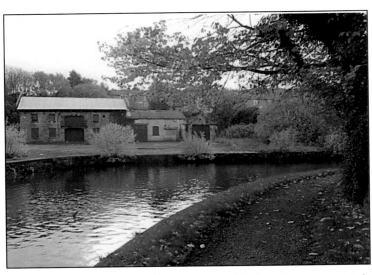

**Figure 24** The Terminus Warehouse visible from the south portal of Turn Bridge

Manchester Road Wharf, once a heavily industrialised enclave, known today as the Weavers' Triangle, received a long overdue makeover. A small museum was opened containing some canal memorabilia and other interesting artefacts related to the textile industry. Some two years later, it was announced that the Terminus Warehouse (known locally as Finsley Gate Warehouse) is to undergo renovation, possibly reverting to public use;

**Figure 25** The start of the Burnley Embankment looking north from beneath Turn Bridge

thankfully much of the waterfront in the vicinity of Burnley town centre may be perceived as an amenity rather than an eyesore.

The Terminus Warehouse (Figure 24) is located between the Weavers' Triangle and Turn Bridge (Figure 25) which is close to where the canal enters the Burnley Embankment. The narrows just visible in the distance indicate the position of the Yorkshire Street Aqueduct.

The rivets to the underside of Turn Bridge offer evidence that the present structure replaced that which was originally built.

The Embankment extends along the straight section of canal shown in Figure 26, the Yorkshire Street Aqueduct being just visible in the distance where the channel narrows.

Figure 27 is the view from a point north of Turn Bridge near to where the River Calder passes beneath the Embankment. Burnley town centre lies to the left of the towpath.

During 1927, the Yorkshire Street Aqueduct (Figure 28), was completely rebuilt to permit the widening of this main east bound thoroughfare, no doubt eliminating a notorious road traffic

**Figure 26** Burnley Embankment viewed from the north parapet of Turn Bridge

**Figure 27**

Looking north along the Embankment towards Burnley town centre

bottleneck. The pedestrians walking along the footpath below offer some idea of the scale of this ambitious structure.

A wharf immediately to the east side of Yorkshire Street Aqueduct shown in Figure 29 is served by a jib crane which would have accessed the lime kilns located nearby.

Figure 30 offers an indication of the significant volume of earth required during the construction of the embankment, which came from the canal cutting to the north of Burnley. Once Robert Whitworth's major involvement in the setting out of the Burnley Embankment was complete, mindful of the fact that he was involved in several other canal schemes elsewhere, he requested that his salary be halved, a virtue which is seldom displayed among executives today! Sadly in March 1799, Robert Whitworth died, whereupon Samuel Fletcher took charge with Whitworth's son William acting in an advisory capacity. This magnificent structure is a worthy 'Wonder' which remains a lasting testimony both to Robert

**Figure 28**

The Aqueduct spanning Yorkshire Street

Whitworth's ingenuity and the sheer endeavour on the part of those responsible for its construction.

**Figure 29**

The jib crane located on the east side of the Yorkshire Street Aqueduct

**Figure 30** Burnley Embankment looking south towards Turn Bridge

# Chapter 3

# Bingley Five Rise Locks
## (Leeds and Liverpool Canal)

When faced with rugged terrain, the early canal engineers sometimes employed 'staircase' locks where two or more locks are constructed contiguously, the tail lock gates of the upper chamber serving as the upper lock gates of the lower chamber, as shown in Figure 31.

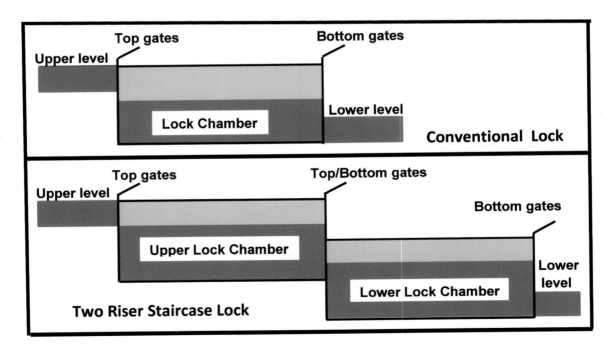

**Figure 31** Conventional and Staircase Locks

Early during the construction of the eastern end of the Leeds and Liverpool Canal, a number of staircase locks was introduced, this design of lock being employed some ninety years previously at Fonseranes on the Canal du Midi in southern France. Without doubt, the most celebrated staircase lock system on the English canal network is the Five Rise Staircase at Bingley. Later, when canal construction resumed after an enforced thirteen year break, the canal company decided that where possible staircase locks were to be avoided on the grounds that they consumed more water than a conventional lock flight. One suspects that this policy was based upon their operational experience in the intervening years. Had the location of the summit level occurred near the mid-point of the canal rather than one third of the distance between Leeds and Liverpool, also had the terrain to the east of the summit resembled that to the west, no staircase locks may have been employed; see Figure 32.

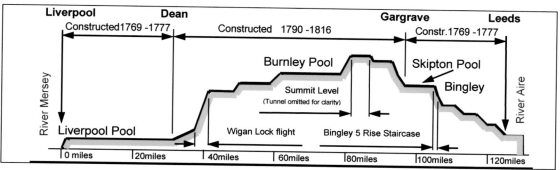

**Figure 32**  The different stages in which the Leeds and Liverpool Canal was constructed

No doubt due to the fact that photography was not available until some eighty years later, there appears to be little available in the way of a pictorial record of the Bingley Five Rise Locks during their construction. The photograph in Figure 33, taken during a

subsequent maintenance closure, offers some indication of the complete structure. Initially the floor of each chamber was constructed using timber, this eventually being replaced using concrete.

**Figure 33**

Bingley Five Rise Locks drained for maintenance purposes, possibly a century after their construction

Records suggest that the lock free section of canal between Skipton and Bingley was completed and brought into use during April 1773, whilst the section of canal from Bingley to Thackley near Shipley, which in addition to the Five and Three Riser Staircase Locks at Bingley employs a Two Riser Staircase Lock system at Dowley Gap, was brought into use during March 1774. Based upon the degree of difficulty in the building of these structures, one is tempted to speculate that the construction team responsible for the lock chambers within this length of canal may well have worked from east to west, attempting the Dowley Gap Two Rise Staircase initially followed by the Bingley Three Rise and finally the Bingley Five Rise Staircase Locks. There is a possibility that each of the staircase lock systems was constructed simultaneously, though it is likely that the available budget may have prevented this. Whilst the source of the stone employed is uncertain, transporting it to the construction site would have been fraught with difficulties. It is possible that those engaged in the construction would not have had the benefit of a fully operational canal to assist with this problem, especially if the stone had been quarried above Skipton, which would have presented a strong case for the construction of the staircase lock systems to proceed from west to east (Bingley to Dowley Gap). As was the case centuries earlier at Stonehenge, the logistics involved in sourcing the materials and transporting them to the construction site rivalled, or possibly outweighed, the building of the structures themselves!

When approaching the Five Rise Staircase from Bingley town centre, one is treated to the view which appears in most of the guidebooks; see Figure 34. Even on a dull November afternoon, this abrupt 18 metre (59 feet) ascent offers a most impressive vista.

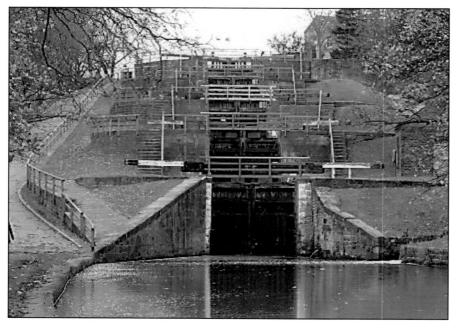

**Figure 34**

Bingley Five Rise
Staircase

**Figure 35** Bingley Five Rise Staircase and by-wash

**Figure 36** The towpath skirting the Bingley Five Rise Staircase

**Figure 37** Looking towards Skipton from the top of the Bingley Five Rise Staircase

As one nears the bottom of the Five Rise Staircase, the impression of its height lessens whilst the building alongside the lower chamber appears more prominent (Figure 35). Though at the time of the photograph the lock gate balance beams were due for a coat of paint, the complex is in good overall condition, considering it was completed in 1774.

Figure 36, showing the walkway alongside the structure, captures its pleasing blend of elegance and utility despite the extensive use of the now mandatory safety rails. The walkers serve to illustrate the sheer size of the structure.

Whilst the area immediately above the Five Rise Locks is not as photogenic as that below, it is still attractive (Figure 37). A number of motor cruisers moor above the swing bridge, shown here next to the hamlet of Oakwood located to the right of the canal. Beyond this point, the canal enters the lock free Skipton Pound, a 28 km (17.5 mile) level having been completed some eleven months prior to the Five Rise Locks, and offering some spectacular Pennine moorland scenery throughout.

The view from above the Bingley Five Rise Staircase depicted in Figure 38 is deceptive when compared to that offered from the bottom gates of the upper chamber, see Figure 39.

Despite the close proximity to the heavily built up Bingley town centre, visible in the distance, the surroundings of the Bingley

**Figure 38** The view from the swing bridge above the Bingley Five Rise Staircase

Five Rise Staircase remain predominantly rural.

The view from the tail end of the upper chamber is spectacular, as depicted in Figure 40, the distant mill chimney being located alongside the Bingley Three Rise Staircase located on the fringe of the town centre.

The Bingley Five Rise Staircase is an unique example of bold canal

**Figure 39** Bingley Five Rise viewed from the bottom gates of the upper lock chamber

**Figure 40**   View from the bridge next to the bottom gates serving the upper lock chamber

construction from early in the canal building era, and some three years after its completion formed part of a truncated length of waterway connecting the River Aire at Leeds with the Pennine village of Gargrave. It would offer prosperity to the surrounding areas from the instant it was opened, thanks primarily to the carriage of limestone from Gargrave to the burgeoning industrial towns and cities within the West Riding of Yorkshire, the length of canal between Thackley and Leeds being completed during 1777. Without doubt, the revenues from these initial cargoes from 1773 onwards helped fund the subsequent completion of the 'missing link' between Gargrave and Burnley (recommended 1790). The extent of this remaining construction work was considerable; consequently the through route between Leeds and Liverpool was not opened until 1816, some forty two years after the Bingley Five Rise Staircase was completed, and some forty six years after the commencement of the canal, when the first sod was cut in Halsall Cutting, west Lancashire.

# Chapter 4

# Standedge Tunnel
## (Huddersfield Narrow Canal)

What on earth led to the construction of a canal tunnel almost 5 kilometres (three miles) long forming the most part of a summit level at an elevation of 198 metres (648.6 feet), within a canal barely twenty miles long through rugged Pennine terrain (see Figure 41) containing no less than seventy four locks? The answer is sought in the following sequence of events.

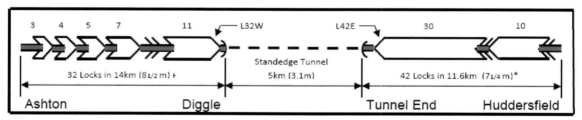

**Figure 41**  The Huddersfield Narrow Canal
(† Scout Tunnel omitted for clarity; * L42E is 1.6km (1m) from tunnel)

As the eighteenth century drew to a close, the industrial revolution had taken hold, triggering a relentless growth in population, manufacture and trade. Despite the groups of towns on either side of the Pennines prospering and beginning to realise the benefits of waterway transport, only one scheme to construct a canal across this chain of hills was being undertaken, namely the Leeds and Liverpool Canal which arced significantly northwards in doing so. Proposals for more direct trans-Pennine routes were mooted in the form of the Rochdale Canal, also an eastern extension of the Manchester, Bolton and Bury Canal (see Figure 42), though in 1792 Bills in respect of these proposals failed in Parliament.

At this time, a Bill in respect of a canal linking the City of Manchester with the thriving town of Ashton-under-Lyne had been passed, and its construction had commenced,

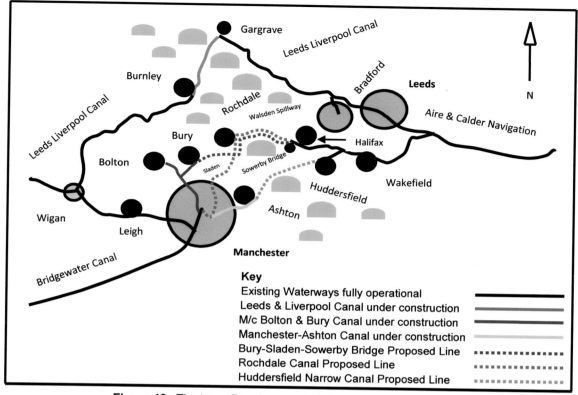

**Figure 42**   The trans-Pennine canal routes proposed during 1792

whilst the Leeds and Liverpool Canal remained far from complete. A new group of promoters which included a significant number of shareholders in the Ashton Canal Company, perceived these circumstances to offer a window of opportunity, realising that employing the Tame Valley to the west of the Pennines, and the Colne Valley to the east, offered the most direct canal link possible between the Lancashire and Yorkshire conurbations, this being considerably shorter (see Figure 42 again) than that proposed by the Rochdale Canal, which unlike the eastern extension of the Manchester, Bolton and Bury Canal, was expected to be authorised.

Construction of the Huddersfield Narrow Canal began in 1794 under the supervision of Benjamin Outram, and in order to achieve the direct route essential for the undertaking to be profitable, the company was forced into building a summit tunnel. Hence, in order to restrict costs, they had no option but to construct a narrow canal. The summit tunnel at Standedge linked the west Pennine village of Diggle with what was later to become the east Pennine hamlet of Tunnel End near Marsden. The construction process was somewhat piecemeal at first, records suggesting that it was not possible to engage a general contractor to undertake the work, the initial and subsequent contracts being in respect of 'labour only', leaving the canal company to provide the necessary management infrastructure in order for work to progress. Predictably, the construction of the tunnel was fraught with difficulties, which were further exacerbated by poor planning, excessive water ingress from the millstone grit, surveying errors and significant under-estimates of the ongoing costs, leading to a chronic lack of funds. Consequently, tunnel construction proceeded somewhat sporadically until late 1806 when the accomplished canal engineer Thomas Telford was summoned to assist. Telford duly expedited the works and the tunnel was opened for navigation during December 1810, although at a cost of £123,804, which was more than double the original estimate provided by Benjamin Outram.

The ongoing difficulties encountered during the construction of the canal were to continue throughout its working life. The rugged terrain, together with the high elevations, led to operational difficulties caused by lack of water supply during the summer months, and the canal frequently becoming frozen in winter. Local mill owners regularly complained that the canal was reducing their water supplies. Added to these difficulties, Standedge Tunnel quickly became a bottleneck due to the fact that despite incorporating passing places, it could take up to four hours for men to 'leg' a boat through it. Following unsuccessful attempts to haul narrow boats through the tunnel using a steam powered tug, the company reverted back to the use of professional 'leggers'. Figure 43 offers an

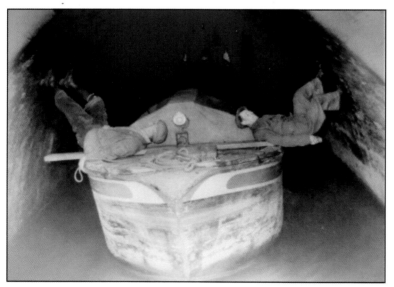

indication of just how hazardous and laborious this process is. During 1813, mindful of all these problems, the canal company sought to encourage agricultural development of the land which flanked the waterway for much of its length. To this end, it provided lime kilns which were fed by limestone via the nearby Peak Forest Canal, whilst reducing its tolls for the carriage of dung and manure. Another

**Figure 43** 'Leggers' moving a loaded narrow boat

initiative pursued by the canal company around this time, was to market the canal as a through route across northern England though this was seriously compromised by the fact that the length of the locks on the adjoining waterways to the east measured 17.5 metres (57.5 feet), some 4 metres (12.5 feet) shorter than those employed on the Huddersfield Narrow Canal. Though a number of short length boats were constructed, their carrying capacity was reduced by around 19%. Thanks to expenditure on improvements to water supplies and ongoing repairs, the company did not pay its shareholders a dividend for its initial years of operation between 1812 and 1824. In 1825, a dividend of £1 per share was paid.

Due to expenditure on additional warehousing, no dividend was paid between 1826 and 1830. From 1830 to 1842, dividends varying between £0.50 and £2.00 per share were paid, after which due to the effect of railway competition, no further dividends were paid. Matters were not helped by its main competitor the Rochdale Canal, with whom the HNC reluctantly reached an agreement on minimum rates for the carriage of cargo. The less direct route of the Rochdale Canal employed the Walsden Spillway, a glacial trough traversing the Pennines, enabling the canal to be constructed at a maximum elevation of 183 metres (600 feet), thereby reducing the number of locks required, and eliminating the need for a summit tunnel (see Figures 41 & 42). In 1836 the attractions of this route were embodied in an Act to build the Manchester to Leeds railway, which was duly completed in 1841. The Rochdale Canal immediately reduced its tolls, discarding its rate-fixing agreements with the Huddersfield Narrow Canal, which had no option but to follow suit. The effect of this policy was to increase traffic on the canal, but with no operational profit yielded thereafter. In 1844, the Manchester-Leeds Railway Company proposed a branch from Cooper Bridge to Huddersfield. This proposal was contested by a newly formed Huddersfield-Manchester Railway Company, which itself proposed a link from Cooper Bridge to Huddersfield, thence to Stalybridge linking with the Sheffield, Ashton-under-Lyne and Manchester Railway. The intent of the Huddersfield-Manchester Railway Company, which eventually won the day, was to employ the same route as the Huddersfield Narrow Canal; consequently both concerns merged, forming the Huddersfield and Manchester Railway and Canal Company, the railway proprietors paying the canal owners £30 for their shares, each of which had a market value of no more than £8! Their generosity is most likely to have been influenced by the estimated £100,000 saving made in the late 1840s, when the canal tunnel was employed during the construction of the rail tunnel running parallel with it. Further cost savings occurred during 1871 and 1894 when the second and third railway tunnels were added (see Figure 44). The short lived Huddersfield and Manchester Railway and Canal Company leased itself to the London and North Western Railway in 1847.

The Standedge Canal Tunnel, hence the Huddersfield Narrow Canal, held great appeal to the railway companies for the reasons summarised below:

i) Those engaged in the design of the three railway tunnels had a datum for both level and direction in place from the outset. The length of the existing canal tunnel would enable an accurate estimate to be made of the lengths of the proposed railway

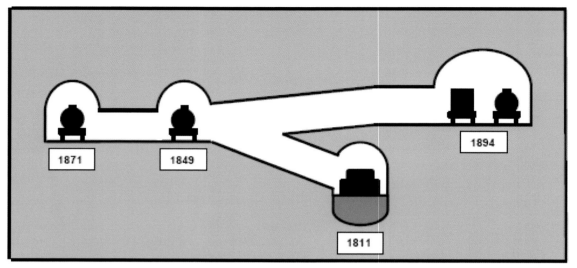

**Figure 44** Section looking west, showing the position of the canal tunnel relative to the three railway tunnels, all of which were constructed at later dates.

tunnels, thereby offering a realistic forecast of their costs which would benefit also from the fact that they were each built level throughout, see paragraph iii) below.

ii) During the construction of the railway tunnels, the canal tunnel would offer a very convenient means of removing the unwanted spoil, whilst allowing transportation of cumbersome items of equipment and volatile materials to and from the work site.

iii) To this day, the canal tunnel offers a means of draining surface water and snowmelt brought into the railway tunnels by trains. During the days when steam locomotives used the railway tunnels, the canal tunnel provided some much needed ventilation for the train drivers.

Despite losing money, the canal continued to be used regularly, and the limited information available suggests that during the latter half of the nineteenth century over 164,000 tonnes (161,000 tons) were conveyed annually. By 1916, the navigation of Standedge Tunnel had become such a rarity as to warrant a mention by the local press who reported that a boat with a cargo of vitriol substitute to a company in Mossley was the first boat through the tunnel in two and a half years. On 6 November 1921, the last recorded boat passed through the tunnel entering at Marsden at 2.30pm and emerging at Diggle at 6.30pm. From this day forward, the canal continued to operate as two unconnected halves, the goods carried dwindling year by year until December 1943, when the London, Midland and Scottish Railway Company having absorbed the London and North Western Railway some twenty years earlier, decided to apply for abandonment, which does not appear to have been successful, because in 1948 when both the railways and the canals were nationalised, the Huddersfield Narrow Canal came under the control of the British Transport Commission. Throughout the decades prior to and after nationalisation, a handful of pleasure boats cruised the 'lock free' upper pounds of the nearby Peak Forest and Macclesfield Canals emanating from Marple.

This intrepid band of pioneer canal pleasure boaters included long-serving train driver Bert Kennerley (see Figure 45), who frequently drove steam trains carrying freight through the Standedge rail tunnels as part of the regular Grimsby to Manchester 'fish runs' during the 1920s when the canal tunnel was still open to commercial traffic. On one occasion, Bert and his fireman were lucky to escape with their lives when allegedly due to a signalling error, they found that when emerging from the tunnel, they were on the same track as an approaching train. Bert and his fireman jumped off their train prior to the resulting collision, thereby avoiding fatal injury. During his later

**Figure 45**   Bert Kennerley and family on board *Royal Oak* in 1946, embarking from High Lane Arm on the Macclesfield Canal

life, Bert together with his wife Edith, son Frank and daughter in law Brenda navigated much of the canal system available to them at the time. This led to Bert becoming an active IWA member, serving as harbourmaster during the National Rally held at Macclesfield in 1953. Sadly, Bert passed away during the late 1970s, before the completion of Huddersfield Narrow Canal restoration, thus he was not able to navigate the Standedge Canal Tunnel which without doubt he would have greatly appreciated! Another pleasure boat plying the Peak Forest and Macclesfield Canals at this time was the wooden motor cruiser *Ailsa Craig*, used during the post war years as a 'day boat' by a family living close by (see Figure 46). The clinker built hull, featuring a low freeboard stern with a transom, suggests that perhaps earlier in her life the craft had been employed as a ship's lifeboat or for estuary fishing. During its conversion for pleasure use, a cabin had been added to the bow of the vessel, with a raised lantern roof section to offer more light within. In 1948,

**Figure 46** *Ailsa Craig* in 1945, embarking from Stypherson, on the Macclesfield Canal

*Ailsa Craig* had been acquired by a boat hire company based in Stone, Staffordshire, from where Robert Aickman, later to be joined by Tom Rolt and their partners, hired her to undertake a campaigning cruise on behalf of the IWA, whereby they would exercise their right to navigate some of the more neglected parts of the canal system, including the Ashton and Huddersfield Canals. This would enable them to highlight the widespread difficulties faced by canal users at the time. Bow-hauling the boat through the initial length of the Huddersfield Narrow Canal (Figure 47) caused damage to her hull, resulting in a serious leak. The torrential rain which prevailed at the time added to these difficulties. All on board attempted to save their possessions, with the exception of Robert Aickman, who doggedly wrote a letter of appeal to the man who was the very head of the waterways. Aickman's response to the problem in this manner would not have helped his

**Figure 47** *Ailsa Craig* in 1948 being bow-hauled into a lock by a gang comprised of British Transport Commission staff shortly after entry to the Huddersfield Narrow Canal

already strained relationship with his far more 'hands on' colleague Tom Rolt, who at the time would no doubt have been preoccupied with ascertaining the extent of the repairs and means to undertake them as expediently as possible. These fundamental differences were to lead to an irreparable and acrimonious parting of the ways some two years later. Nevertheless, Aickman's both vehement and impassioned plea resulted in repairs being undertaken to their vessel by two shipwrights seconded from Merseyside who, under the direction of a local BTC canal foreman named Wilf Donkersley, ensured that *Ailsa Craig* was able to resume the eastward ascent towards Standedge Tunnel the following day!

Figure 48 captures a truly defining moment during the early days of the Inland Waterways Association's campaign. Faced with this level of adversity, many would abandon their efforts, turn back and accept defeat graciously, especially considering that those involved were undertaking this campaigning cruise in their own time and at their own expense. Not only did the Rolt-

**Figure 48** *Ailsa Craig* secured whilst lying within one of the Huddersfield Narrow Canal lock pounds, which had been drained to enable repairs to her hull

Aickman party tough it out, but upon re-boarding their patched up wooden hire boat, they promptly headed for the longest canal tunnel in the country which had not been navigated for over a quarter of a century! Understandably, Wilf Donkersley the BTC foreman who monitored *Ailsa Craig*'s ongoing progress, and whose assistance had proved invaluable at the time, was fondly remembered by all the crew many years later.

Prior to entering the tunnel (Figure 49), those on board *Ailsa Craig* were Aickman, Rolt and his wife Angela, IWA Secretary Elizabeth Jane Howard, IWA Treasurer James Sutherland and his wife Anthea. The higher freeboard possessed by the motor cruiser in comparison with that of the work boats (even when they were not loaded), meant that the tunnel roof was struck on a number of occasions, arresting forward motion, whereupon Tom Rolt reversed the boat in order to release her, then selected forward gear and full speed to force her through these tight spots. To navigate the canal tunnel would

**Figure 49** *Ailsa Craig* immediately prior to entering the tunnel at Diggle with Tom Rolt at the helm, along with the IWA party. A last minute check is being undertaken on the propeller!

have exposed the *Ailsa Craig* to the steam egress from the locomotives travelling through the adjacent railway tunnel consequently as they inflicted considerable damage to the lantern roof. To add to these difficulties, steam trains were in use whilst they were navigating the tunnel, consequently as they encountered the connecting passages which occur at regular intervals, visibility could be drastically reduced in an instant. When the boat finally emerged from the tunnel at Marsden, all on board had black faces! Nevertheless, against all the odds *Ailsa Craig* with her hardy band of campaigners on board made the very last private boat passage through Standedge Tunnel just prior to the closure of the Huddersfield Narrow Canal.

Subsequently British Waterways (the successors to the BTC), who assumed control of the canal and responsibilities for the upkeep of water supplies, had their staff navigate the tunnel annually for inspection purposes, using one of their work boats moored nearby.

During the late 1950s and early 1960s, the adjoining Ashton and Lower Peak Forest Canals were under serious threat of abandonment, whereupon a concerted restoration campaign was launched by the IWA. This campaign succeeded during 1974, and has since been deemed to be one of a series of milestone restoration campaigns heralding the way for further equally ambitious projects elsewhere in the country.

Commencing around 1974, an equally vigorous restoration campaign was undertaken by the fledgling Huddersfield Canal Society, which no doubt mindful of the difficulties which occurred during the restoration of the Ashton and Lower Peak Forest Canals, was quick to gain both the approval and backing of the local authorities through which the canal ran, namely Kirklees, Oldham and Tameside. Understandably, recovering what had initially been built as a low budget canal running through unprecedented rugged terrain for most of its course was at the time dubbed the Impossible Restoration. Against many seemingly insurmountable difficulties, the canal and its summit tunnel were officially reopened to navigation during 2001, representing a testimony to all those involved over a period of almost thirty years!

A boat trip through the canal tunnel today enables one to fully appreciate the efforts of those who were armed with the fortitude to build it, and also the resolve of the men who 'legged' fully loaded boats through it and later, those involved in restoring it. The original Tunnel Keeper's cottage at Tunnel End, which was well-used during the restoration of both the canal and the tunnel, is now employed by the Canal &

**Figure 50**   The Canal & River Trust trip boat berthed at Tunnel End near Marsden has a much lower freeboard than the *Ailsa Craig*

River Trust trip boat operators for their kit storage and mess facilities, also as a café, appealing to those using the trip boat and others visiting the Tunnel End area out of interest (Figure 50). Evidence of the railway track which runs parallel to the canal at this point is visible above the canal tunnel portal. Nearby, in the direction of Marsden, there is covered canal dock and warehouse converted to offer a visitor centre, offering a wealth of information on the canal, an exhibition of tunnel and canal memorabilia, and also a craft workshop where on occasions hand weaving is demonstrated.

Figure 51 indicates the surprisingly good condition of the brickwork forming the tunnel arch. The members of CRT staff, who offer commentary throughout the trip, are both helpful and very well briefed, pointing out details of how the tunnel was constructed.

**Figure 51** The CRT trip boat is well into the tunnel, now relying entirely on artificial light

**Figure 52** A CRT staff member monitoring progress from one of the 'adits'

Passengers have the option of riding in the aft cockpit shown here, or within the illuminated saloon.

Figure 52 illustrates how land based CRT staff are able to liaise with the trip boat at regular intervals by employing the access passageways, or adits, which interconnect with the nearby rail tunnels, one of which has been converted to accommodate a rough terrain road vehicle used to continually track the passage of craft navigating the canal tunnel. Clearance in the canal tunnel is very low, at times, and one may appreciate why Tom Rolt resorted to physically forcing *Ailsa Craig* through, despite damaging her superstructure in the process! Well into the tunnel, the bore breaks through into a natural cavern; see Figure 53. This must have offered something in the way of respite to those engaged in its construction, not to mention the relief that would have been felt by those on board the *Ailsa Craig*!

Upon arrival at the berth near the west end of the tunnel near to Diggle (Figures 54 and 55) the CRT staff are on hand to assist the passengers with their

**Figure 53**

At this point in the tunnel, the bore has broken through into a natural 'cavern'

disembarkation prior to their transfer back to Tunnel End near Marsden by minibus. The appeal of this unique excursion was such that the trip boat was immediately loaded with a different group of passengers who had travelled from Tunnel End riding in the same minibus in order to make the return east bound boat trip.

**Figure 54** Two hours after entry, the western end of the tunnel approaches

Of the three canals which traverse the Pennines, the Huddersfield Narrow Canal would have been by far the most ambitious undertaking. In places, this lengthy summit level tunnel is almost 200 metres (650 feet) below the land surface. In contrast, on the Leeds and Liverpool Canal summit level, the 1.5 kilometres (1640 yards) long Foulridge Tunnel is dug much closer to the land surface. In fact, some 677 metres (740 yards) of this tunnel reverted to a 'cut and

**Figure 55** The CRT trip boat moored at the west portal of the tunnel

cover' method of construction due to difficulties encountered when attempting to drill the bore. As explained earlier, the Rochdale Canal summit level does not feature any tunnel whatsoever, though its relatively short summit level (1.2 kilometres or 1320 yards) running through the Walsden Spillway gorge is often short of water.

Considering the rather turbulent history of the Huddersfield Canal during its construction, operation and protracted restoration, together with the ongoing challenges presented by the unique Standedge Tunnel, it is a near miracle that both the waterway in its entirety and the tunnel especially are available for all to enjoy today.

# Chapter 5

# Anderton Lift
## (Trent and Mersey Canal - River Weaver)

Approaching its northern end, the Trent and Mersey Canal runs alongside the Weaver valley (Figure 56), thence to a junction with the Bridgewater Canal at Preston Brook via three tunnels, each of which may be navigated in one direction at a time only, creating a series of bottlenecks when this was a working canal. Also, in order to transfer goods between Preston Brook and the port of Liverpool, a five mile length of the Bridgewater Canal at its western end provided a link with the Mersey Estuary. When used by all of the Trent and Mersey Canal traffic together with the Bridgewater Canal traffic to and from the Manchester area, this short length of canal became exceptionally busy, consequently during 1828, the ten locks within the Runcorn flight were duplicated in an attempt to reduce delays.

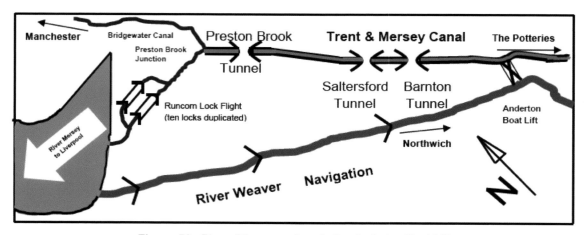

**Figure 56** Plan of the area close to the Anderton Boat Lift

Near to the Cheshire village of Anderton, the Trent and Mersey Canal runs very close to the River Weaver Navigation, assuming a level some 15.3 metres (50.3 feet) above it. Thus, at this point in 1872 it made good commercial sense to consider the transfer of water-borne freight between these two waterways, thereby bypassing the three tunnels and the busy Runcorn Lock flight. Furthermore, each of the three sizeable locks on the River Weaver Navigation below Anderton was able to accommodate a number of canal narrow boats simultaneously.

Due to the abrupt change in levels at this point, a canal link employing locks (even a lock staircase) was impractical. Prior to the construction of the Lift, the time saving benefits of this route were already being realised, thanks to the gravity-assisted chutes used to feed salt from the canal to the river; these remained in use long after the Boat Lift was introduced.

The above factors yielded what is arguably the world's first successful boat lift, a truly unique and ground breaking structure. The original design employing water-based hydraulics was simplicity in its self, making use of two caissons or large tanks moving in opposite directions to transfer boats vertically between the canal and the river, the base of each caisson being connected to a hydraulic ram. The two hydraulic rams were linked by an inter-connecting pipe containing a control valve. Figure 58 overleaf shows two pairs of narrow boats in transit, one pair having entered the caisson descending from the canal level,

**Figure 57** Anderton Lift (electrically operated, pre-1983), with a Claymoore Navigation hire boat emerging, after having descended from the Trent and Mersey Canal to the River Weaver  *Waterway Images*

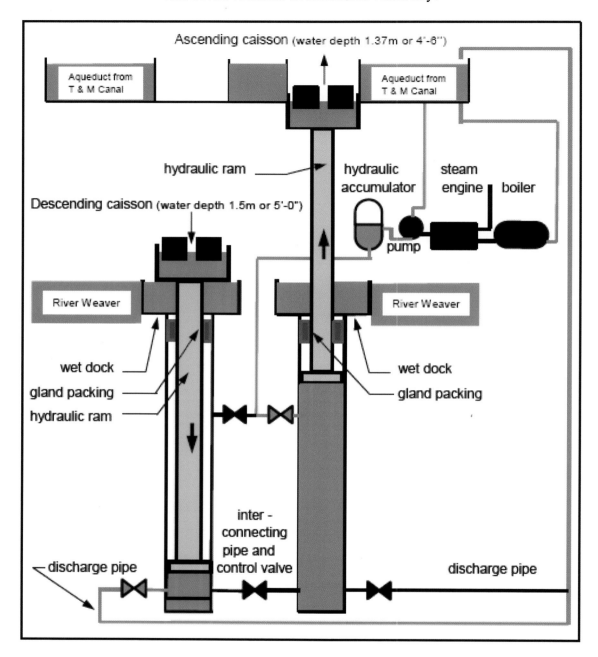

**Figure 58**  Schematic diagram of the water based hydraulic system originally employed by the Anderton Boat Lift at the instant the 'power assisted' lift stage commences

the other pair having entered the caisson ascending from the river level. The two way motion having been triggered by opening the valve in the inter-connecting pipe, whereby the left hand caisson which was slightly overfilled, began its descent, the hydraulic ram beneath it retracting, causing water to transfer into the hydraulic ram beneath the right hand caisson, which began its ascent.

Subsequently, when the descending caisson came into contact with the river, the ascending caisson had covered 90% of the distance between the River Weaver and the Trent and Mersey Canal, some 1.2 metres to 1.5 metres (four to five feet) short of the canal level without any power being expended whatsoever! To achieve the final 10% of the required lift motion, the valve in the inter-connecting pipe was closed, whilst the discharge valve serving the ram beneath the descending caisson was opened, whereupon the ram beneath the ascending caisson was supplemented by a volume of pressurised water from a hydraulic accumulator, until each caisson assumed the opposite position to when the lifting process began (see Figure 58 again).

Finally, each pair of narrow boats exited their respective caissons, thus completing the two way transfer between the River Weaver and the Trent and Mersey Canal.

This prototype structure, undoubtedly well ahead of its time, made use of the best design practices and construction techniques available during the late nineteenth century. The Engineer responsible, Edward Leader Williams (who as explained earlier in Chapter 1, was knighted in 1895) enlisted the help of Edwin Clark, an established civil engineer with extensive experience of hydraulic lifting machinery within a maritime environment. Although records suggest that the Boat Lift operated relatively trouble free for its first ten years, unforeseen difficulties often emerge when such ground-breaking designs are introduced. The Anderton Boat Lift was no exception, in that it was designed and built at a time when our 'in depth' understanding of different engineering materials and the manner in which they interact within a corrosive environment was limited. This requires both an appreciation of the molecular composition of the materials together with effective methods of testing them, prior to, during and following extensive service. (We now term such knowledge and practice 'materials science', but sadly this technology was just emerging at the time).

These factors resulted in operational difficulties so severe that those responsible for the Boat Lift's operation had no option but to make fundamental changes to the manner in which it functioned. In short, thanks in no small part to the extensive industries lining the nearby canal and river, the excessive chemical content of the water used to operate the Lift was so detrimental to its wellbeing, that around 1896 a condensing plant was introduced. This modification gave a twofold improvement, in that it offered a source of clean water for use with the Boat Lift Hydraulics, whilst providing sufficient energy savings to reduce the operating costs of the steam engine. Also at this time, a small dynamo and battery were adopted in order to supply electric lighting and power for the warehouses, wharf cranes and the Boat Lift gates, saving the labour costs of three men hitherto in constant deployment.

These arrangements continued until 1902, when the boilers, which had suffered extensive internal corrosion, were condemned on the grounds of safety, whereupon it was decided to replace them with an electrically driven hydraulic pumping plant powered using mains electricity. Whilst this arrangement offered cost savings compared with the steam plant, the costs of repairing the hydraulic rams and associated pipework in order to guarantee safe, trouble-free operation were continually increasing. In 1904 the Weaver Navigation Trustees were alerted to the gravity of the situation, thanks to a report compiled by their engineer Colonel J.A. Saner, who advocated that the Boat Lift be completely rebuilt on its existing 'footprint' to enable conversion from hydraulic to electrical operation, whereby both the caissons would be suspended from above and raised using two 40kW (30hp) electric motors. Whilst this would offer the advantage of each caisson being able to function independently, counterbalance weights had to be employed to assist with their lifting, hence additional structural steelwork would prove essential. The additional load on the Lift structure imposed by this new mode of operation meant that the foundations would need to be upgraded. The eminent engineer Sir Benjamin Baker approved the proposals submitted by Colonel Saner, albeit with some detailed modifications, resulting in working drawings being prepared and tenders for the proposed work being invited by late 1905.

Mindful of disruption to through traffic, hence the potential loss of much needed revenue, Colonel Saner arranged for the reconstruction of the Boat Lift to employ three planned stoppages occurring over a two year period as follows: between 6.00pm on Thursday 12 April and 6.00am on Monday 30 April 1906, using relays of men working day and night, an area beneath the lift measuring 24 metres (80 feet) by 12 metres (39 feet) was excavated to a depth of 1.5 metres (5 feet) to permit the construction of a dry dock for the caissons to descend into. The original wet dock arrangement was bottomless, consisting merely of side and end walls. The dry dock was formed by constructing a concrete invert nominally 1.5 metres (5 feet) thick, reinforced by a number of rolled steel joists each measuring 305 millimetres by 153 millimetres (12 inches by 6 inches). This was tied in to the side and end walls, which in turn were underpinned. The second stoppage between 4.00pm on Saturday 4 August and 7.00am on Monday 13 August 1906 allowed the frame and fore bay for the new river gates to be installed, thereby completing all the submerged works. Following this stoppage, additional overhead steelwork complete with wheels and shafting, together with new ancillary equipment, were added whilst the lift was operational. The third and final stoppage occurring between Thursday 16 April and Thursday 5 May 1908, enabled the east caisson to be completed and commissioned, along with some repair work to the aqueduct. Thereafter, all hands were employed in the completion of the west caisson, which became fully operational by late July 1908, heralding the completion of a truly amazing sequence of events. The lengths of the two intervals between the stoppages may have been extended due to difficulties revealed during the course of each of the first two stoppages.

Figure 59 depicts the three 'fathers' of the Anderton Boat Lift who are (from left to right) Edward Leader Williams, the proposer and conceptual designer, Edwin Clark, who was responsible for its detail design and construction, and Colonel J.A. Saner, who between 1905 and 1908 carried out extensive redesign and retrofitting work to enable the lift to be converted to electrical operation, thereby ensuring its survival. The mural, located close to the visitor centre, is accompanied by an interpretation plaque explaining how the role of the lift has changed since its completion in 1875 to the present day.

**Figure 59**    The visitor centre mural in honour of the three 'fathers' of the Anderton Lift

Between 1908 and 2000, the field of hydraulics improved almost immeasurably. In addition to aeronautical and automotive applications, it has proved invaluable to large scale engineering projects such as the Thames Barrier, which relies on hydraulics for its operation, and the Millau Viaduct in France which employed hydraulics to enable its erection.

Thanks to oils developed specifically for hydraulics, corrosion problems leading to accelerated wear are a thing of the past. Ongoing improvements in mechanical seal technology have offered improved performance, reliability, component longevity and 'user friendly' materials in comparison with traditional gland packings.

The Lift continued to rely on electrical operation until eventually it fell into disrepair and closed in 1983. Heritage Lottery Funding enabled it to be rebuilt between 2000 and 2002, a condition of this restoration work being that it was converted back to hydraulic operation. Modern hydraulic oil, rather than water, is employed as the hydraulic fluid; see Figure 60.

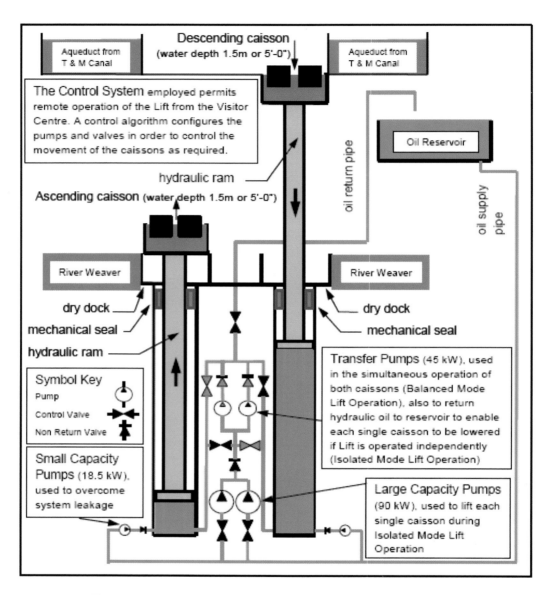

**Figure 60** Schematic diagram of the oil based hydraulic system now employed by the Anderton Boat Lift shortly after the Balanced Mode Lift Operation has commenced

A ride on the Anderton Boat Lift in its present form is likely to convince anyone that the conversion from electrical back to hydraulic operation is wholly justified. Not only is the ride quiet and smooth, the power expended is minimised; also, the load on the structure has been reduced significantly thanks to the removal of the balance weights which are unnecessary!

In conclusion, the Anderton Boat Lift, known by some as the 'Cathedral of the Waterways', offers an excellent example of bold Victorian engineering. One suspects that most of those who visit the Boat Lift or navigate it are unlikely to appreciate the 'blood, sweat and tears' which were necessary to design, build, maintain and update this facility to offer future generations the opportunity to enjoy a truly unique and exhilarating experience.

**Figure 61**

The Anderton Boat Lift in 2015, following the resumption of hydraulic operation

**Figure 62**

The Anderton Boat Lift viewed from the bank of the River Weaver

# Chapter 6

# Pontcysyllte Aqueduct

literally: 'the bridge that connects'

## (Llangollen Canal)

Sir Walter Scott once described this structure as 'the stream in the sky', and 'the most impressive work of art I have ever seen'. There is certainly no doubt that the building of the Pontcysyllte Aqueduct owed much to the expertise, flair and imagination of the country's top canal engineers. Yet even today, precisely how the planning and construction of the aqueduct unfolded is unclear. There follows an attempt from limited archive material to piece together what occurred.

The two prominent engineers involved were Thomas Telford (1757-1834) and William Jessop (1745-1814). To understand how the construction of the aqueduct was made possible, one must delve into the career history of these two individuals. It was however the Whitchurch born architect William Turner who conducted the initial surveys of the canal, which included plans for high level

**Figure 63** Pontcysyllte Aqueduct, opened in 1805, from the Trevor end
*Waterway Images*

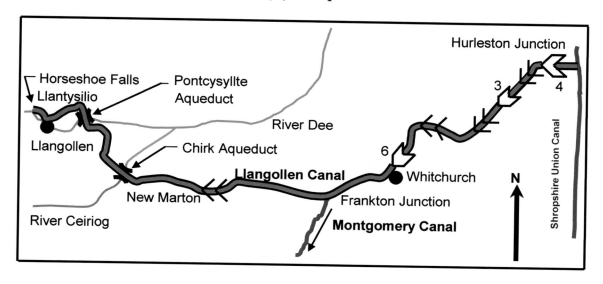

**Figure 64** The Llangollen Canal, as built

aqueducts at Pontcysyllte and Chirk, spanning the Dee and Ceiriog valleys respectively (Figure 64). These high level aqueducts would allow water to be drawn from the River Dee at Llantysilio, above Llangollen, Clwyd, in order to supply the whole 46 miles of canal running east to Hurleston in Cheshire, where it joined the Chester (now Shropshire Union) Canal. This has ensured that the Llangollen Canal is never short of water, (some of which is drawn off and stored above the Hurleston Lock flight in order to supply the needs of the Crewe area to this day). Whilst we will never know for certain that this concept was the intention of Turner, the howls of derision that greeted his original plans (especially from those of a Welsh persuasion) suggest that it was, and he knew precisely what he was doing!

Thomas Telford's early career was rich and varied. He served an apprenticeship as a stonemason, and worked on the building of Somerset House. He was then employed in Bath by Sir William Pulteney, the MP for Shrewsbury, also the richest individual in Britain at the time. Upon successfully completing his work in Bath, he became the Surveyor of Public Works for the county of Shropshire, where many of the early iron foundries were located.

William Jessop's family was blessed with engineering pedigree. His father worked under the celebrated Civil Engineer John Smeaton during the building of the Eddystone Lighthouse, but sadly died when William was sixteen years old. At this time, Smeaton became his guardian, taking him on as his pupil and later his assistant, giving him invaluable canal surveying experience whilst still in his early twenties. By 1793, Jessop, then in his late forties, was enjoying a successful career serving as Principal Engineer both for the Grand Junction Canal and the Ellesmere Canal (more recently known as the Llangollen Canal). It was in this latter role that he appointed Telford as one of his assistants.

In 1795, following the death of Josiah Clowes, engineer to the part-built Shrewsbury Canal, Telford was appointed by this canal company as his successor. At Longdon-on-Tern, Clowes had attempted to build a masonry aqueduct, incorporating small brick arches, but it was swept away by floods. Telford opted to replace most of the structure with a cast iron trough and supporting structure, which would offer far less restriction to the river flow, together with the benefits of a far more favourable strength to weight ratio (Figures 65-70). In approving Telford's design, the company directors who were predominantly Shropshire Iron Masters, had brought their influence to bear, thereby offering him the requisite experience of working with cast iron that would subsequently serve him well at Pontcysyllte.

The cast iron navigation trough, measuring 2.1 metres (7 feet) wide, is fabricated in four sections each measuring approximately 14 metres (47 feet) long. Figure 69 shows the non-towpath side of the aqueduct, and the course of the river usually runs below the third trough section from the left. Clearly the resistance to flow during flood conditions is far less than that offered by a masonry structure. Each trough section consists of a series of wedge shaped castings each bolted together in a similar manner to that later to be employed at Pontcysyllte.

**Figure 65**  The south side of Longdon-on-Tern Aqueduct, where the end of the cast iron trough overlaps the surviving abutment of the original masonry aqueduct.

**Figure 66**  Longdon-on-Tern Aqueduct viewed from the east end. The structure appears in very good condition despite some signs of neglect

**Figure 67**  Longdon-on-Tern Aqueduct viewed from the west end. The towpath is formed using a narrow low depth trough which is bolted to the main navigation trough

**Figure 68**  The east end of Longdon-on-Tern Aqueduct, clearly showing the original masonry abutment built by Clowes. Telford's cast iron central section was used to replace the masonry arches, swept away during floods

Early in 2016, the Longdon-on-Tern Aqueduct appeared in good condition. It is a Grade I listed structure and also a Scheduled Monument.

Erected in 2003 during the building of the M6 Toll Motorway, a modern day version of this aqueduct spans the carriageway between Lichfield and Brownhills in Staffordshire. This structure, which resembles Telford's original Longdon-on-Tern aqueduct, will in the future serve the Wyrley and Essington Canal. Ironically, both these aqueducts, which are currently devoid of water, are each located on the lines of canals which are in the throes of restoration.

**Figure 69**  Longdon-on-Tern Aqueduct viewed from the east bank.

**Figure 70**   The underside of Longdon-on-Tern Aqueduct indicating how the towpath trough is bolted to the main navigation trough

A month before Telford's success at Longdon-on-Tern, Outram had completed a single span cast iron aqueduct on the Derby Canal at Holmes, close to the centre of Derby. Both Outram and Jessop were partners in the company responsible for its manufacture, namely the Butterley Iron Works, located close to the Cromford Canal, a waterway which had been engineered by Jessop. Thus, around 1795, Telford and Jessop's careers were converging.

Figure 71 shows the Holmes Aqueduct, which ran beneath a road bridge that was built directly over it, probably at a later date. The Pegg's Flood Lock visible beyond the aqueduct places this location around five and a quarter miles along the Derby Canal from its junction with the Trent and Mersey Canal at Swarkestone.

Around 1945, commercial traffic ceased on the Derby Canal, which fell into decline, whereupon in 1971 the world's first cast iron aqueduct was dismantled (see Figure 72), stored and later, as a result of what appeared to be a breakdown in communication, unintentionally scrapped.

Though the planning, design and manufacture of both the Holmes and the Longdon-on- Tern Aqueducts would have occurred during the same time period, despite Telford and Jessop both being involved in the Ellesmere Canal and Jessop's close association with Outram, the information currently available suggests that these structures, which were located some sixty miles apart, were each conceived, developed and constructed as completely separate entities. Furthermore, each structure

**Figure 71**   The Holmes Aqueduct, Derby

**Figure 72**   The Holmes Aqueduct during dismantling

is quite different, in that the Longdon-on-Tern Aqueduct serves a narrow canal traversing a river valley located in spacious rural surroundings, in complete contrast to the Holmes Aqueduct which serves a broad canal crossing a brook located in confined, heavily urbanised surroundings.

Thus, at the end of the eighteenth century, we have an intriguing situation involving two eminent canal engineers working on behalf of the Ellesmere Canal, both acquainted with cast iron, and both mindful of the fact that in order to cross the River Dee whilst avoiding locks down to and up from a low level masonry structure, a high level aqueduct was needed at Pontcysyllte, possessing a high strength to weight ratio. Though we can not be certain who made the decision to employ a trough section using cast iron rather than masonry, it is possible that Jessop, who was in overall control, endorsed Telford's detailed proposals. Though undoubtedly he was strongly influenced by Telford's success at Longdon-on-Tern, Jessop, who at the time was engaged on many other canal building projects all around the country, would have had a vested interest in promoting the more widespread use of cast iron at every possible opportunity, considering his connections with the Butterley Iron Works.

The work of the accomplished Shropshire iron founder William Hazeldine (1763-1840) proved to be invaluable to Telford and Jessop in this venture (Figure 73) in that he was responsible for the manufacture of the cast iron plates and arched support castings used to construct the aqueduct. In order to manufacture many of these components, locally, thus avoiding their costly transportation over lengthy distances, Hazeldine took out a long term lease on land between nearby Trevor and Cefn-Mawr in order to set up the Plas Kynaston foundry, located around half a mile from Pontcysyllte. Despite the relatively close proximity of the foundry, it would appear that the transportation of the heavy castings relied upon a tramway system to supply the aqueduct site. Figure 74 shows the Trevor Arm which currently serves as a hire base. The small arch beneath the right hand bridge abutment originally accommodated the tramway which once served the Plas Kynaston Foundry.

The railings beyond the parapet wall above the tunnel shown in Figure 75 indicate the boundary of the now demolished Monsanto Chemical complex, most of which during

2017 occupied a restricted area.

This tunnel marks the starting point of the Plas Kynaston Canal which appears to have been dug after the completion of the Aqueduct and progressively infilled to around 2005. From its starting point, this canal headed in a dead straight line in the direction of the Plas Kynaston Foundry maintaining the 95

**Figure 73** Thomas Telford, William Hazeldine and William Jessop

metre contour of the Llangollen Canal summit level. This very strongly suggests that the line of the Plas Kynaston Canal occupied the route of the tramway used in the building of the aqueduct a few years earlier.

**Figure 74** The Trevor Arm at the north end of the Aqueduct

**Figure 75** The tunnel marking the start of the Plas Kynaston Canal at the end of the Trevor Arm

During the present day it is very difficult to pinpoint the exact location of the Plas Kynaston Foundry which is now demolished, together with the chemical complex which succeeded it. Figure 77 offers an indication of its approximate location close to what in 2017 is the Flexsys Social Club next to the hamlet of Abernant. Thus, after casting, fettling and drilling, at Plas Kynaston the trough sections were, following transportation by tramway, assembled at the aqueduct site as required. It is also likely that during the construction phase, a section of tramway was installed along the aqueduct towpath itself (Figures 78 and 79). This must have been a sophisticated operation on the part of Hazeldine (whose almost 'magical'

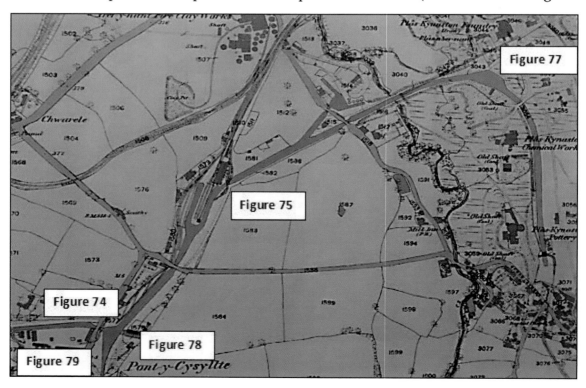

**Figure 76** The Trevor Arm and Plas Kynaston Canal linking Trevor with Cefn-Mawr

**Figure 77** The approximate location of now demolished Plas Kynaston Foundry in 2017

abilities earned him the nicknamed 'Merlin') and his team, involving a customised foundry, no doubt employing the use of quality control, standardisation, design for manufacture and design for assembly techniques, each of which are now commonplace

**Figure 78** The trough overlapping the north abutment nominally twelve feet wide, the towpath being cantilevered over it

**Figure 79** During construction the towpath may well have incorporated a tramway

within the field of production engineering, but nothing short of ground-breaking at the time!

The towpath to the north end of the Pontcysyllte Aqueduct (the bottom left of Figure 78) is a continuation of that located to the right (south) side of the Trevor Arm shown in Figure 74.

The Aqueduct consists of nineteen sections of cast iron trough, each nominally 16 metres (53 feet) long, 3.7 metres (12 feet) wide and 1.5m (5 feet) deep, comprising of a number of castings bolted together resting upon four arched support ribs (see Figures 80 & 81).

Whether Hazeldine was responsible for the manufacture of the nuts and bolts employed to fasten the sections together is unclear, but to this day the joints are watertight. Without doubt the cast iron plates would need to be accurately pre-drilled within the foundry workshop before despatch to the site.

Though the sequence in which the assembly was undertaken is uncertain, as the foundry is located nearer the north end of the emerging structure, it would be far easier for the men under the direction of Hazeldine to assemble and install the first trough section between the north abutment and the first masonry support column, working southwards, one trough section at a time. Also, the installation of each successive trough section would offer a working platform gradually extending southwards across the Dee valley to Froncysyllte.

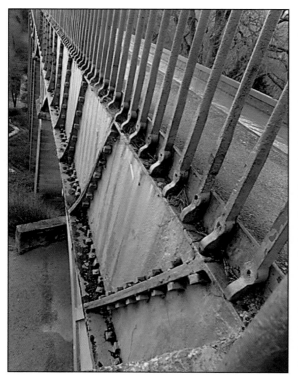

**Figure 80**  The attention to detail of each of the cast iron trough sections is evident here.

Prior to trough assembly, the four cast iron support arches would need to be positioned, each of which is supported by, and let into, the masonry. The stonemasons would have some form of scaffold in place to enable them to proceed with their construction from either the ground or the river bed, which couldn't have been easy, especially bearing in mind the volume of water involved: the River Dee falls some 38 metres (120 feet), during its eight kilometre (five mile) journey from Llangollen. Near to the top of each support column, the stonemasons would have to liaise very closely with the ironworkers to achieve the desired outcome. Without doubt this would have been easier said than done!

Each of the two centre support ribs appear to be a 'one piece' casting (Figure 81), which one suspects would need to be positioned prior to the two outer side arches, again one piece castings, support being provided by the masonry column. It is uncertain whether or not the longer arched castings were produced locally, or supplied from one of Hazeldine's Shropshire foundries.

With the installation of each successive trough section, undoubtedly those involved with the construction would introduce ways of making the operation more efficient. Placement and securing of the arched ribs and side arches would offer a working platform to enable assembly of the trough sections.

Figure 81 Arch support ribs which would be positioned prior to the trough being assembled

At the time it was opened, a permanent tramway across the aqueduct was proposed to transport goods. Perhaps the fact that the potentially volatile chemicals and fragile products, which were manufactured in considerable volume within factories to the east of the Trevor Arm, dissuaded this idea, in that transportation of these cargoes, particularly

Figures 82 and 83 Both these views of the north abutment serve to indicate an elegant, functional design reflecting standardisation, uniformity and good quality castings

**Figure 84** 'Big oak trees out of little acorns doth grow!' Despite being completed in 1805, to this day the Pontcysyllte Aqueduct remains an elegant, well-proportioned structure sitting at ease with its surroundings, unlike some of our modern day structures!

across the aqueduct, was far safer and more effective by boat, where sudden jolts are avoided.

The Pontcysyllte Aqueduct and the surrounding area are now classed as a World Heritage Site, and quite rightly so. There is a number of amenities on offer to accommodate visitors to the Aqueduct site, both at Trevor (north end) and Froncysyllte (south end), where ironically the A5 road linking London with Holyhead, which Telford commenced improving some five years later in 1810, passes close by.

The overall condition of this neighbourhood in the present day is a far cry from the immediate post war years, when most of what is now the Llangollen Canal was barely navigable. We owe a huge debt of gratitude to a handful of pioneering pleasure boaters, namely the co-founder of the IWA, Tom Rolt, on board his converted narrow boat *Cressy* and the Grundy family, on board their cruiser *Heron*, who drew attention to the plight of this waterway, which has thankfully been fully reclaimed. Perhaps in a few years, the currently infilled Plas Kynaston Canal may undergo similar improvements, which would breathe much needed life into the post-industrial area sited between Trevor and Cefn-Mawr, whose present day condition is in much need of both remediation and regeneration.

Subject to funding availability, the not too distant Montgomery Canal - currently the subject of a long term restoration initiative - will be restored to full navigable status. This, together with a fully restored 1.2 kilometre (1320 yard) Plas Kynaston Canal would certainly help to ease the chronic overcrowding which prevails on the Llangollen Canal each summer, particularly along its western summit level, such is its unprecedented attraction to pleasure boaters.

**Figure 85**  Visitor facilities near to the Pontcysyllte Aqueduct

# Chapter 7
# Devizes Lock Flight
## (Kennet and Avon Canal)

The idea of linking London with Bristol by means of two river navigations and a canal was first mooted during Elizabethan times, inspired no doubt by the fact that near to their sources in South Gloucestershire, the Thames and the Bristol Avon are at one point a mere three miles apart. Other factors in support of this idea were the poor state of the roads, also the threat posed to coastal craft travelling between these two seaports by both French Navy warships and the privateer 'opportunist' vessels which plied these waters. Though a canal was proposed by Henry Briggs around 1626, it was not until the late 18th century that the plans which yielded the Kennet and Avon Canal in its current form finally materialised. These were preceded around sixty years earlier by John Hannah's improvements to both the Kennet Navigation (a tributary of the Thames) and the Avon

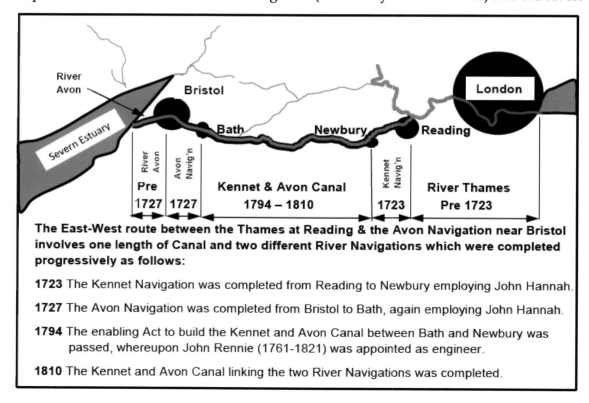

The East-West route between the Thames at Reading & the Avon Navigation near Bristol involves one length of Canal and two different River Navigations which were completed progressively as follows:

**1723** The Kennet Navigation was completed from Reading to Newbury employing John Hannah.

**1727** The Avon Navigation was completed from Bristol to Bath, again employing John Hannah.

**1794** The enabling Act to build the Kennet and Avon Canal between Bath and Newbury was passed, whereupon John Rennie (1761-1821) was appointed as engineer.

**1810** The Kennet and Avon Canal linking the two River Navigations was completed.

**Figure 86**   Plan of the 'coast to coast' waterway route from the Thames to the Severn

Navigation. When opened early in the nineteenth century, the Devizes Lock flight was the final length of the Kennet and Avon Canal (hence the east - west route) to be constructed; see Figures 86 & 87.

John Rennie was an accomplished civil engineer who favoured broad canals, hence his aqueducts at Dundas and Avoncliffe on the Kennet and Avon Canal (and also over the River Lune on the Lancaster Canal), are truly spectacular. His lock flight at Devizes, which raises the canal 72 metres (237 feet) in 5.3 kilometres (2 miles), undoubtedly a challenging civil engineering project, represented the final link in the length of canal to be completed as part of a waterway envisaged some two hundred years earlier. Often when major construction projects near their conclusion, the funding becomes scarce, resulting in enforced measures to realise cost savings. This does not appear to have happened on the Kennet and Avon Canal; moreover one could say that the Devizes lock flight represents a testimony both to John Rennie's ingenuity, also his refusal to compromise his designs in order to yield cost savings. Sadly, it is likely that the Devizes lock flight will for ever remain the 'poor relation' to some of the other iconic structures such as Tower Bridge and the Clifton Suspension Bridge which occur elsewhere along this 217 mile 'coast to

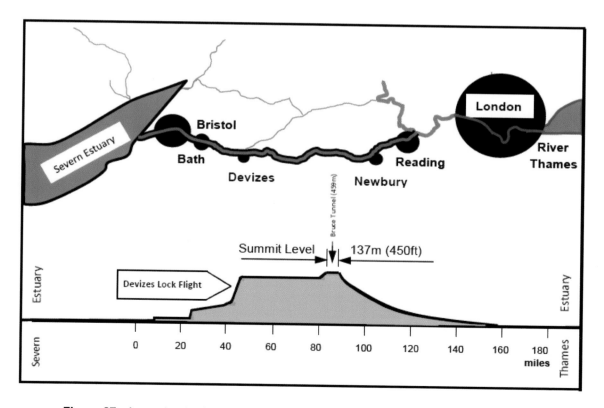

**Figure 87**   Approximate plan & sectional view of the route from the Thames to the Severn

coast' waterway running from the mouth of the Bristol Avon to the commencement of the Thames Estuary; see Figure 87.

During the construction of the Devizes lock flight, the towpath alongside accommodated a horse drawn railway which was used between 1801 and 1810 to carry freight between the operational lengths of canal above and below the lock flight (see Figures 96 & 97). Without doubt at the time, this facility would also be employed to convey building materials as and when required. In 1810 the opening of the Devizes lock flight enabled the first barge to navigate the Kennet and Avon Canal in its entirety, resulting in the cost to carry goods from London to Bath reducing to £2-9s-6d per ton (£2.44 per tonne), which compared favourably to the cost of goods carried by road, which varied between £6-3s-0d and £7 per ton (£6.06 and £6.90 per tonne).

By 1816, the Kennet and Avon Canal Company had purchased the adjoining river navigations, thereby controlling the stretch of waterway from Bristol to a point east of Reading where the Kennet enters the Thames, which may have reduced the unit carrying costs even further. Shortly afterwards in 1818, the K & A Company employed a fleet of around seventy barges, each having a capacity of 61 tonnes. The majority of the freight they handled consisted of stone and coal emanating from the Somerset Coal Canal. By 1832, some 300,000 tonnes of freight was carried annually, generating an income of £45,000. These figures, together with the need in 1821 to install gas lighting along the Devizes lock flight, suggest that boat movements would continue during the hours of darkness. A relatively short period of success continued until 1841, when the canal's prosperity came under threat from the Great Western Railway Company, whose route virtually replicated it. In 1851, the Kennet and Avon Canal Company sold out to the GWR, resulting in an ongoing decline in its fortunes which was hastened by an extremely harsh policy on the part of the railway company, which deliberately set about to eliminate the canal company. During 1906, tolls levied on its canal were fifty percent higher than any other comparable waterway in the country. Fires were prohibited within moored work boats, thus during winter live-aboard boatmen suffered extreme hardship unnecessarily. Each weekend between Friday evening and Sunday evening, all craft were forbidden to navigate the canal, making pleasure boating impossible. Above all, maintenance was both neglected and under-funded, cheap unsuitable wood being used in the repair of lock gates. Not surprisingly, the last through passage made by a boat occurred during 1951, just prior to closure.

Thankfully, a vigorous rear-guard action was staged over many decades by a stoic group of canal enthusiasts, each possessed with sufficient vision and resolve to resist further decline of their adopted waterway and later to actively engage in its restoration. In 1946, when the Inland Waterways Association was formed, the Kennet and Avon Canal

**Figure 88**   Part of the Caen Hill Lock Flight during the early nineteenth century, prior to the effects of the neglectful policies inflicted whilst under Great Western Railway ownership.

featured among its prominent campaigns. Shortly afterwards in 1949, the IWA's Kennet and Avon Branch was formed, some two years or so in advance of the canal being closed to navigation between Bristol and Reading on safety grounds.

However, late in 1950, just as the IWA began to gather support, it suffered a major internal policy clash concerning canals under the threat of closure. Some members wished to prioritise these threatened canals on the grounds of 'usefulness', whilst other members strongly disagreed with this approach, claiming that the IWA should campaign to 'save every single mile of canal under threat'. Matters came to a head in 1951, when many of the 'prioritise' faction including the co-founder Tom Rolt, together with former Vice Chair and prolific canal author Charles Hadfield, resigned their membership. A further consequence of this rift was the loss of the IWA's Kennet and Avon Branch, resulting in the formation of the Kennet and Avon Canal Association to continue to resist closure, which thankfully later during this year, successfully defeated proposals to abandon the canal. In 1962, the Kennet and Avon Canal Association was replaced by the Kennet and Avon Canal Trust, which later worked  in conjunction with British Waterways, the IWA and its colleagues within the Waterways Recovery Group (see Introduction) on restoration projects using volunteer labour. During 1990, following much in the way of avid campaigning, fund raising and volunteer work parties, the canal was re-opened during a ceremony performed by Her Majesty the Queen at a point between Locks 43 and 44 on the Caen Hill section of the Devizes flight; see Figure 89.

The difficulties encountered during the lengthy restoration of this canal no doubt resembled those experienced during its initial construction. Ongoing improvements proved necessary, including the installation of a back pumping station at Devizes locks in 1996 at a cost of £1 million supplying water at a rate of 379 litres/sec (300,000 Imperial gallons per hour).

**Figure 89**  An early view of the canal below Caen Hill Lock 44, where some 100 years later, on 8 August 1990, HM Queen Elizabeth II reopened the Kennet and Avon Canal shortly after its restoration was completed.

The Devizes flight of twenty nine locks in total occurs in three stages, the Kennet and Avon locks being numbered from west to east; see Figure 90. The lower (west) end of the flight commences just below Foxhangers Cottage, with seven irregularly spaced locks (Locks 22 – 28). These are followed by the sixteen closely grouped Caen Hill locks spanning the middle of the flight (Locks 29 – 44), and finally the six irregularly spaced locks at the top of the flight approaching the town of Devizes (Locks 45 – 50).

The town of Devizes lies to the right of the canal beside the Locks near to the summit; see Figure 91. The replacement lock gate balance beams differ slightly from the originals (see Figures 88 and 89), in that they incorporate a slight bend at the point where they intersect the gates.

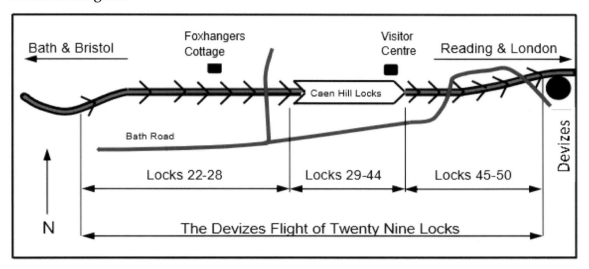

**Figure 90**   Plan view of the Devizes Lock Flight in its entirety

**Figure 91**   Lock 44, the top of Caen Hill Locks. The distant Lock 45 is the first of the six irregularly grouped locks leading to the summit of the Devizes Lock Flight

The uncanny resemblance between the two photographs in Figure 90 serves to illustrate the uniformity of the design and construction of the locks employed within this flight.

The view from Lock 42 shown in Figure 93 and Figure 94 below illustrates the considerable width of the side pounds employed between each Lock. This is an attempt

**Figure 92**   Two views looking down Caen Hill Locks: Lock 43 appears
on the left whilst Lock 42 appears on the right.

**Figure 93**   Looking down the Caen Hill lock flight from Lock 42

to mitigate the effects of potential water shortages during heavy usage, especially within the pounds between the sixteen closely spaced locks occurring within the Caen Hill Flight. Figure 95 offers an indication of just how much restoration work went into this lock flight, which was in a near derelict state as recently as the 1970s.

**Figure 94**   The view from Lock 42 looking northwards to Roundway Hill

**Figure 95** Symmetry personified! The Caen Hill Lock Flight as it appears today

England's most celebrated lock flight, the Caen Hill section of Devizes Locks (Figure 96) is unique to the British canal system, in that the closely grouped locks are built in a dead

**Figure 96** Caen Hill Locks viewed from below Lock 29

straight line. The pedestrians shown here on the towpath are walking the route of the temporary railway used whilst the locks were being constructed. The attention to symmetry, clean lines, appealing proportions and the absence of elaborate fine detail are

**Figure 97** Looking east from the towpath arch beneath the bridge at the tail of Lock 28. The temporary railway would have run under the bridge at this point

reminiscent of the art deco style of architecture which did not emerge until over a hundred years later. The extent of the uniformity of these locks suggests that the stone masonry, lock gates, paddle gear and access bridges appear to have been standardised, hence interchangeable, thus offering considerable cost savings during manufacture, construction and upkeep.

Sadly this canal epitomises the unique sequence of events which unfolded within what is now the United Kingdom and Ireland during the nineteenth century due to the end of the 'canal era' being overlapped by the coming of the steam railways, whereupon many of our thriving waterways were very soon forced into advanced states of decline; see Footnote.

Many pleasure boaters make a point of navigating the Kennet and Avon, heading westward to Bath or Bristol before returning by the same route. After arriving at Bristol, other more ambitious boaters choose to return via the River Severn. One cannot fail to be impressed by this waterway especially its *pièce de résistance,* namely the truly spectacular Caen Hill Locks section of the Devizes lock flight. We should never forget the hard work of the many volunteers involved in the preservation and restoration of the Kennet and Avon Canal, which has allowed boats to visit this part of the country, and to enjoy the numerous features on offer, designed by John Rennie and fashioned by his sizeable team of master craftsmen.

**Figure 98**   'Live-aboard' and 'live-ashore' boaters berthed at Foxhangers, below Lock 27

**Figure 99**   Looking down the Devizes flight from Lock 26. The lock in the middle distance is the first of four locks at the lower end of the flight

# Footnote

This book has sought to review the 'Seven Wonders of the Waterways' originally perceived by Robert Aickman, which as explained in the Introduction, were used in order to draw attention to our much neglected canal network in the immediate post-war period.

In comparison with other countries, the development of our canal system and its subsequent demise was unique. Within the seventy year period spanning the late eighteenth and early nineteenth centuries, when most of our canals were constructed, the age of steam power had arrived. The Rainhill Trials, where Stephenson's *Rocket* demonstrated the viability of steam powered locomotives, occurred during 1825 when our later canals were still incomplete. During the overlap between the canal and steam railway systems within most developed countries, the legislature in place usually took steps to prevent railway companies buying up canals, which though already well established were allowed to develop and expand further. In this country however, when a railway company promoted a Bill in Parliament seeking to construct its railway, inevitably it encountered opposition from a canal company already operating within the same district. In these instances, Parliament encouraged the railway company to buy off and buy out the canal company often at a 'knock down' price. In this manner, the railway companies acquired around a third of the waterways, whose distribution were such that control of virtually all the system fell into their hands. The ruthless manner in which the Great Western Railway treated the Kennet and Avon Canal as explained in Chapter 7, was replicated by other railway companies on other canals to varying degrees.

Though our waterways were not abandoned, much of the freight they carried was transferred to the railways, which often ensured that canal tolls were increased to unrealistic levels, whilst considerably underfunding their upkeep. A deliberate policy of 'neglect and silence' on the part of the railway companies was considered simpler and cheaper than abandonment.

In May 1947, the fledgling IWA challenged the Great Western Railway to provide a safe and clear passage along the then semi-derelict North Stratford Canal in order to realise the statutory right to navigation which was in existence at the time. When Tunnel Lift

Bridge near Kings Norton had collapsed due to overloading by road vehicles, the 'temporary' fixed steel low level structure used to replace it effectively closed the canal. The GWR had agreed to raise the fixed structure upon any notice of 'intended passage'. This materialised when Tom Rolt's narrow boat *Cressy* navigated the waterway, though not without ongoing difficulty. Later that year around two thirds of the inland waterways system was nationalised, whereby control was assumed by the British Transport Commission. Whilst it was hoped that the Commission would rescue the waterways from their neglected state, many of these nationalised waterways received considerably less maintenance than when they were under the control of the railway companies. The pre-nationalisation difficulties prevailed on some of the more neglected waterways, as was explained in Chapter 4 when in 1948 the cruiser *Ailsa Craig* with Tom Rolt and Robert Aickman on board managed to navigate the Huddersfield Narrow Canal, though not without extreme difficulty.

Thankfully during the intervening seventy years, the overall picture has changed both dramatically and favourably in the form of waterway restoration, re-opening and the acceptance of their remarkable potential for leisure use. This has led to all Seven Wonders being operational during 2017, but what does the future hold for each of these iconic structures? A brief review follows.

| Wonder Title | Full Address | Visitor Facilities |
| --- | --- | --- |
| Barton Aqueduct | 601 Barton Lane, Eccles, Manchester M30 0HX | None offered |
| Burnley Embankment (Manchester Road Wharf) | Manchester Road, Burnley, Lancs. BB11 1JG | Partial |
| Bingley Five Rise Locks | Beck Lane, Bingley, West Yorkshire BD16 4DS | None offered |
| Standedge Tunnel | Waters Road, Marsden, Huddersfield HD7 6HQ | Visitor Centre |
| Anderton Boat Lift | Lift Lane, Anderton, Northwich, Cheshire CW9 6FN | Visitor Centre |
| Pontcysyllte Aqueduct | Station Road, Trevor Basin, Wrexham LL20 7TG | Visitor Centre |
| Devizes Lock Flight | CRT Car Park, The Locks, Devizes SW10 1QR | Visitor Centre |

Despite the **Barton Aqueduct** and its surroundings holding much in the way of interest to canal enthusiasts worldwide, no indoor visitor facilities are offered, which is a great pity. A facility of this nature, fully equipped with displays, artefacts and visual aids would both capture and reveal precisely what occurred at Barton from the initial involvement of James Brindley and the Duke of Bridgewater to the present day.

Close to the south end of the **Burnley Embankment** is Manchester Road Wharf, which has undergone a full restoration with safe car parking, and accommodates a Museum dedicated to the surrounding district and containing some canal artefacts. Whether the redevelopment of the nearby Terminus-Finsley Gate Warehouse close to the south end of the Embankment will include any visitor facilities, remains to be seen.

At the summit of the **Bingley Five Rise Locks** there is a CRT Office with information for boaters, and a café nearby. Car parking is limited hereabouts, though the mill building next to the Three Rise Locks, below, which has been converted to a retail outlet, has a car park.

Should a visit to the Burnley Embankment or the Bingley Five Rise Locks be proposed, it is worth enquiring beforehand whether the traditional Leeds & Liverpool short boat *Kennet* (see below) is on one of her occasional visits. If so, the experience would be greatly enhanced.

There is a visitor centre at the Marsden end of **Standedge Tunnel**, and a well-equipped Museum and Craft Centre with car parking nearby.

The **Anderton Boat Lift** site accommodates a modern purpose-built visitor centre with a good selection of exhibits and a wealth of information, together with an extensive car park.

At the north end of the **Pontcysyllte Aqueduct** there is a modern purpose-built visitor centre containing information relating to its construction, with car parking nearby.

There is a small CRT visitor centre near to the summit of the **Caen Hill** locks (Lock 44) with extensive car parking nearby.

Many of those responsible for our present day waterways and their dedicated staff are assisted by a fully mobilised army of willing, committed and able volunteers capable of a range of support functions including canal reclamation and maintenance, training in bricklaying, lock operation and also fund raising for both canal restoration schemes and deserving charities.

A number of praiseworthy initiatives is presently being undertaken, which may further heighten public awareness. For example, some waterway reclamation and upkeep schemes now involve young people working towards Duke of Edinburgh Awards, former armed forces personnel undergoing rehabilitation programmes and some less fortunate members of society who are offered the wherewithal to acquire and develop new skills following transgressions. Schools are factoring heritage into their curricula, which may extend to museum visits, or the opportunity to venture on board former working boats, perhaps containing interpretation material augmented by original artefacts. In many instances, people are devoting their leisure time in order to deliver these initiatives, a notable example being the short boat *Kennet* and her hardy band of volunteers known as The Friends of Kennet, who regularly ply the Leeds and Liverpool Canal (Figures 101 and 102).

Following a full restoration by volunteers, *Kennet*'s hold now accommodates a floating exhibition chronicling her history, complemented by artefacts, some generously donated by the descendants of those who worked the canal boats, thereby offering an invaluable educational resource which covers the 204km (127 mile) long Leeds and Liverpool Canal.

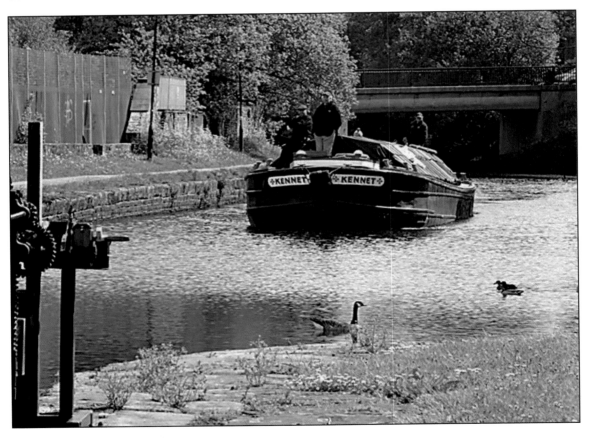

**Figure 101**  The fully restored Leeds & Liverpool short boat *Kennet* approaching Blackburn top lock, in May 2016. Skipper Lynton Childs is at the helm, along with a volunteer crew

**Figure 102** *Kennet* descending Blackburn Locks, during a Sunday morning in May 2016. Though vandals had drained one of the pounds on this flight overnight, lock wheeler volunteers resolved this problem prior to *Kennet*'s arrival

Among the many restoration challenges currently being addressed, easier access to the much under-used Fenland waterways is proposed from the canal network at both Boston and Milton Keynes. Also, a short branch from the Leeds & Liverpool Canal main line originally serving the centre of Bradford is proposed for restoration, which would offer the scope to offer much improvement to a long neglected inner city area. The long derelict Derby Canal, which passes close to Derby city centre, currently undergoing restoration, will offer the considerable benefits of an operational waterway both to the many visitors and those city dwellers living nearby who are currently denied this asset. Furthermore, if built, the futuristic and ground breaking Derby Arm Boat Lift, a key component in the Derby canal restoration, designed by the accomplished professional engineer Alec Dodd (yet another volunteer!), would rank alongside both the Falkirk Wheel and the London Eye as a novel large scale working structure with major tourist appeal. Who knows, the way things are headed perhaps the twenty first century may well yield Seven 'New Age' Wonders of our Waterways!

On a lighter note, our canal restoration schemes are sympathetic to wildlife, which is of great benefit to all. A fully restored section of the Montgomery Canal at Aston bears

**Figure 103** 'People friendly' Mallard and chicks 'canal side'

**Figure 104** A Cormorant 'canal side' awaiting its next meal

**Figure 105** A Heron 'surveying its territory' during an early April morning

testimony to this. It is said that 'the best things in life are free' and though this well worn saying is often hard to believe, some of the occupants of canal habitats bring much pleasure to those who have the good fortune to be in the right place at the right time; see Figures 103 to 105.

Thankfully, the urbanised well populated post-industrial areas served by many of our canals benefit greatly from their presence, in that usually they offer scope for low cost leisure activities such as walking, canoeing and fishing. Some residents are 'adopting' lengths of the canal towpath with the blessing of CRT, which one suspects is to the benefit of everyone.

Enjoy our waterways, whether you walk them or navigate them by boat, dinghy, canoe, kayak, or paddle board, and don't forget to take along your camera!

John Suggitt
Marple Junction
December 2018

# Bibliography
## and Further Reading

Inland Cruising, G. Westall. *1908, Lander Westall & Company*

The 'Engineer' *(Late of 33 Norfolk Street, Strand, London WC2) 24 July 1908*

Know Your Waterways, R. Aickman. *Circa 1960, Press Books Limited*

The Story of Our Inland Waterways, R. Aickman. *1955, Pitman*

Canals in Colour, Anthony Burton & Derek Pratt. *1974, Blandford Press London*
ISBN 0-7137-0715-1

Canal, Anthony Burton & Derek Pratt. *1976, David and Charles (Publishers) Limited*
ISBN 0-7153-6932-6

The Archaeology of Canals, P.J.G. Ransom. *1979, World's Work Limited*
SBN 437-14400-3

Lost Canals and Waterways of Britain, R. Russell. *1983, Sphere Books Limited*
ISBN 0-7221-7652-0

Narrow Boat *, L.T.C. Rolt. *1984, Methuen London Limited*
ISBN 0-413-45550-5

The Shell Book of Inland Waterways, H. McKnight. *1987, Redwood Burn limited*
ISBN 0-7153-8239-X

The Great Days of the Canals, A. Burton. *1989, Tiger Books International PLC*
ISBN 1-85501-695-8

Pennine Passage, a History of the Huddersfield Narrow Canal, M. & P. Fox. *Circa 1990*
*Huddersfield Canal Society*
ISBN 0-9514270-0-8

The Leeds and Liverpool Canal, Mike Clarke. *1994, Carnegie Publishing Limited*
ISBN 1-85936-013-0

British Canals *, Charles Hadfield. *1998, Alan Sutton Publishing Limited*
ISBN 0-7509-1840-3

The Times - Waterways of Britain, J. Mosse. *2013, Times Books Group Limited*
ISBN 978-0-00-793387-7

Green and Silver *, L.T.C. Rolt. *2015, CanalBookShop*
ISBN 978-0-9574037-5-8


www.fairfields.co.uk/sectors/moving-structures/anderton-boat-lift

**Other Books by the Author**

The Marple Lock Flight and its Lost Railway – a canal walk through time

The Reluctant Ex-Patriot – living and working in the Middle East during the 1980s


\* The latest editions of these books are available from www.canalbookshop.co.uk